Quality In Healthcare

OrangeBooks Publication

1st Floor, Rajhans Arcade, Mall Road, Kohka, Bhilai, Chhattisgarh 490020

Website:**www.orangebooks.in**

© Copyright, 2024, Author

All rights reserved. No part of this book may be reproduced, stored in a retrieval system, or transmitted, in any form by any means, electronic, mechanical, magnetic, optical, chemical, manual, photocopying, recording or otherwise, without the prior written consent of its writer.

First Edition, 2024
ISBN: 978-93-5621-799-7

QUALITY IN HEALTHCARE

DR. P. M. BHUJANG
DR. DHANANJAY D. MANKAR

OrangeBooks Publication
www.orangebooks.in

Preface

About fifteen years ago, the then Dean of School of Health Services at Tata Institute of Social Sciences (TISS), Mumbai Dr. C.A.K. Yesudian requested me to take a few lectures on Quality in Health Care to a batch senior medical officers of District Hospitals of Maharashtra as part of a World Bank Project. That was when I got initiated to study and teach the subject to MHA and DHA courses for several batches. Fascinated by the subject, I have been its student.

When I searched in the libraries, I could not find a suitable book on Quality in Health Care covering the syllabus, especially in the Indian context. So, to help the students, I prepared the notes and progressively refined them over the years for distribution among the students. Fortunately, in recent years, several books on the subject by eminent authors have been published.

I am aware that Quality is a vast subject and there are books on each of the major topics. Continuous progress is being made in the field and to keep pace with the advancements is not easy.

During the last one decade, many hospitals in India have been opting to get Accreditation. The establishment of National Accreditation Board for Hospitals and Healthcare Providers (NABH) has created the needed awareness. Since then, many hospitals have received its accreditation. This is also facilitated by the requirement from Insurance Companies to get certification. Thus, there is now a pronounced interest and effort to provide accredited quality health care in India. This book is an effort to present some relevant topics.

I have collected the material from different sources - the majority of which are from internet. I am thankful to all the authors. In a strict sense it is not a text book. It is only a book introducing the different topics. Quality is the goal and there are many different methods and paths to achieve the same. So, at times, it may appear that there is some repetition which perhaps is inevitable. Hope it will be useful to students of quality and inspires them to study and practice subject in greater detail. I welcome suggestions for improving the next edition.

I thank my co-author Dr. Dhananjay Mankar for inspiring and guiding me. I am also thankful to my colleague Mrs. Kshama Chaulkar who has painstakingly and patiently typed the manuscript. My earlier secretary Mrs. Sumati Mohan, who had typed the initial version, too deserves specific mention.

September 2024
Dr. P. M. Bhujang

Contents

Preface v
1. Quality - Concept And Definition 1
2. Evolution Of Quality 4
3. Some Terms And Definitions 7
4. Continuous Quality Improvement (CQI) 11
5. Quality Gurus 12
6. Quality Management System 19
7. Plan – Do – Check - Act (PDCA) Cycle 25
8. Paradigm Shift - In Last Few Decades 29
9. Japanese Management 31
10. American Management 32
11. Quality Circle (Q.C.) 48
12. Quality Circle in a Nutshell 52
13. Just In Time (Jit) 64
14. Jidoka 69
15. Business Process Re-Engineering 75
16. Quality Function Deployment (Qfd) 78
17. Value Engineering (Ve) 80
18. Education And Training 82
19. Leadership 84
20. Cost Of Quality 87
21. Quality Audit 90
22. Legal Compliance And Quality Management 92
23. Licensing, Certification, Accreditation And Awards 93
24. Accreditation 94

25. Quality In Service Sector 95
26. Quality In Health Care 98
27. Measuring Healthcare Quality - Challenges 107
28. Evolution Of Quality In Health Care 113
29. Importance Of Measuring Quality Of Care 117
30. Importance And Benefits Of Quality In Hospitals 119
31. How To Set Up Quality Management Systems 121
32. Credentialing And Privileging 126
33. Clinical Algorithm 128
34. Statutory Compliance For Hospitals 130
35. Risk Management 133
36. Patient Safety 137
37. Ensuring Patient Safety 143
38. Infection Control 146
39. Medical Error 148
40. Medication Error 150
41. Patient Rights 152
42. Performance Measure And Evaluation 154
43. Health Quality Indicators 156
44. Patient Assessment As Per Joint Commision On Accreditation Of Healthcare Organisation (Jcaho) 160
45. Patient Satisfaction 162
46. Assessment Of Public Health Care 165
47. Assessment Of Indicators Of Indoor Services 168
48. Third Party Recognition 177
49. International Standard Organisation (ISO) 178
50. Joint Commission On Accreditation Of Health Care Organizations (JCHAO) 187
51. Joint Commission International (JCO) 189

52. Getting Started 191

53. National Accreditation Board For Hospitals And
Healthcare Providers (NABH)....................................... 192

54. Nabh - Pre Accreditation - Entry Level - Certification................. 196

55. National Accreditation Board For Testing And
Calibration (NABL)... 197

56. ISQUA 199

57. Australian Commission On Safety And Quality In Health Care .. 202

58. Future Of Quality In Health Care 208

References 210

Quality - Concept and Definition

Quality is a word everybody knows but cannot explain properly. Quality holds a different meaning to different people and different connotations to the same person at different times.

The word is derived from Latin word "Qualis", which means, 'Such as', thing really is.

The quality of something depends on the criteria being applied to it. Something might be good because it is useful, or because it is beautiful. or simply because it exists. With the passage of time, concept of quality is also likely to change. Many times, it signifies peculiar and essential character or a distinguishing attribute. Some people view quality as 'performance to standards', others view it as 'meeting the customers needs' or satisfying the customer.

Some more common definitions of quality are:

- Conformance to specifications, measure, how well the service or product meets the specifications e.g., Dimensions of machine part by its design engineers as 3 ± 0.5 inches. Similarly, the wait for room service may be specified as 20 minutes. Good quality must satisfy the predetermined specifications. Conformance to specifications is measurable, though it may or may not be related to customer's idea of quality tasks.

- Fitness for use focusses on how well the product performs its intended function or use. For example, an expensive car and a jeep both meet a fitness for use. If one considers transportation as the intended function. However, if the definition becomes more specific and assumes that the intended use is for transportation on mountain roads, Jeep has a greater fitness for use. Thus, fitness for use is a user-based definition.

- Value for price paid. It combines economics with economics with consumer criteria. It assumes that definition of quality is price sensitive. A client's expectations are different when he eats in a five-star hotel and ordinary restaurant. The client may be more satisfied with the food in that restaurant.

- Support Services – Quality does not apply to the product or service itself, it also applies to people, processes and organization associated with it.

- Psychological criteria – is a subjective definition that focusses on the judgmental evaluation of what constitutes product, or service quality. Different factors contribute to the evaluation such as the atmosphere of the environment or the perceived prestige of the product.

For example, a hospital patient may receive average healthcare, but a friendly staff may leave the impression of high quality. Similarly, some products as associated with the excellence. e.g., Rolex watch, Mercedes car.

Characteristics of Quality

A. Measurable Attributes Dimensions Composition Specification Purity

B. Non-Measurable Attributes Tastes Appearance Customer Appeal Service Sales Support

The above characteristics may be classified in two dimensions

Must-have quality – nearly to fitness for use and conference to specifications

Attractive Quality – what the customer loves but has not specified. Products and services must meet the following requirements.

- Satisfy a well-defined specification
- Meet customer's expectations
- Comply with applicable regulations and standards
- All this at a price which will yield profit for the supplier and considered reasonable by customer.

Quality - Definitions
British Standard:

The totality of features and characteristics of an entity (product or service) that bear on its ability to satisfy the stated and implied needs (of the customer).

Edward Deming:

Good quality does not necessarily mean high quality. It means a predictable degree of uniformly and dependability at a low cost with a quality suited to the market.

American Society for Quality:

A subjective term for which each person has his or her own definition. In technical usage quality can have two meanings.

- The characteristic of a product or service that bear on its ability to satisfy stated or implied needs.

- A product or service free of deficiencies.

Evolution Of Quality

Quality is not a new concept. It existed for centuries. The great sculptures, the ancient monuments, pieces of art are all examples of quality. There were many places and the families which produced exclusive quality products. One such example was /is the famed *Mal Mal* silk fabric from Dacca - which could be folded and packed in a match box. The famed quality watches and books from Switzerland are another such example. This was the period where buyers relied on skill and reputation of the craftsmen. Product inspection was by consumers.

In 13th Century, craftsmen began organizing into unions called as guilds. In this model, young boys learnt a skilled trade while serving as apprentices to a master, often for many years.

Since most craftsmen sold their goods locally each had a tremendous personal stake in meeting customer's needs for quality. If quality needs were not met, the craftsman ran the risk of losing customers, not easily replaced. Therefore, masters maintained a form of quality control by inspecting goods before sale. This model continued to function until the early 19th century.

After the Industrial Revolution, the factory system came into practice. This system began to divide the craftsman's trades into specialized tasks. This forced craftsman to become factory workers and forced shop owners to become production supervisors. It marked an initial decline in employees' sense of empowerment and autonomy in the workplace. Unlike in the past, the number of products manufactured was also large. It also crated competition. To see the products the manufacturer had to produce quality products, at a competitive price. The common practice at that time was:

- Written specifications for materials finished goods and inspection were determined
- Inspection of Incoming goods was carried out.

Non-conforming products were either re-worked or scrapped. It was more a process than a preventive process.

This was the prevalent system in the industrialized world. However, late in 19th century the United States broke from this tradition and adopted a new management approached by Frederick Taylor. His goal was to increase the productivity without increasing the number of skilled craftsmen. He achieved this by assigning factory planning to specialized engineers, by using craftsman and supervisors, who had been displaced by the growth of factors, as inspectors and managers who executed the engineer's plans. His approach led to remarkable rises in productivity, but it had significant drawbacks.

To remedy the quality decline, factory managers created inspection departments to keep defective products from reaching customer. Quality was the responsibility of the inspectors rather than that of production managers.

During this period a separate inspection department was in vogue with a chief inspector. With the erection of this department there came now services and issues e.g. Standards tracing, recording data and the accuracy of measuring equipment. It became clear the responsibilities of the chief inspector were more than just product acceptance and to address defeat prevention emerged. At one time however, electric company had 5200 inspection people out of 40,000 workers.

The beginning of 20th century marked the inclusion of processes in quality practices. Walter Schewart, a statistician for Bell laboratories began to focus on controlling processes making quality relevant not only for the finished product but for the processes that created it. He recognised that industrial processes yield data. He determined that this data could be analysed using statistical technique to see whether a process is stable and in control or if it is being affected by special causes that should be fixed. His concepts are referred to Statistical Quality (Process) Control (SQC or SPC). His work was later developed by Deming. After entering World War II, the US enacted a legislation to help gear the civilization economy to military production. At that time military contracts were awarded to the manufacturer that submitted the lowest bid. Products were inspected on delivery to ensure conformance to requirements.

Since quality was an important safety issue, they started inspecting the units where the arms ammunition and other supplies were produced. Since it was cumbersome, they began to use sampling inspection to replace unit by unit inspection. With the aid of industry consultants particularly from Bell Laboratories they established the standards for suppliers. The army also helped the suppliers by importing them training to improve quality.

After the Second World War, Japan's Industrial System was destroyed. They rebuilt it by using quality management practices with the help of some notable quality gurus – like Juran, Deming and Feigen Baum. They were able to produce, cheaper and high-quality products.

In 1969, the term 'Total Quality' was used first time and it referred to wider issues such as planning, organization and management responsibility. The terms 'Total Quality Control' or Companywide quality control were used, to describe how all employees, from top management to the workers, must study and implement in quality control.

The quality revolution in the West was slow to follow and did not begin until early 1980's. Total Quality Management (TQM) became the centre of these practices in most of the organization.

The British Standard (BS) for Quality Systems had been published in 1979 and in 1983 Natural Quality Campaign was landed using BS 5750 as its main theme. The aim was to bring to the attention of industry the importance of quality for competitiveness and survival in the world market place.

Since then, the International Standard Organization (ISO) 9000 has become the internationally recognised standard for quality management system.

TQM is now part of a much wider concept that addresses overall organizational performance and recognises the importance of process. There is also extensive evidence that demonstrates the benefits from approach.

In to 21st Century, TQM has developed in many countries into holistic framework, aimed at helping organization achieve excellent performance, particularly in customer and business results. In Europe a widely adopted framework is the so called "Business Excellence' or 'Excellence' model promoted by European Foundation for Quality Management (EFQM) and in the UK by the British Quality Foundation (BQF).

Some Terms and Definitions

Quality System: Organizational structure, procedures, processes and resources needed to implement quality management.

Quality Policy: The overall intentions and direction of an organization with regard to quality, as formally expressed by top management.

Quality Planning: Activities that establish the objectives and requirements for quality and for the application of quality system elements.

Quality Management: All activities of the overall management function that determine the quality policy, objectives and responsibilities and implement them by means such as quality planning, quality control, quality assurance and quality improvement within quality system.

Quality Assurance (QA): All the planned and systematic activities implemented within the quality system and demonstrated as needed, to provide adequate confidence that an entity will fulfil requirements for quality.

It refers to the systematic post-production checks, inspections or reviews done to ensure quality of a product or service.

Modern Quality Management Systems: consider quality assurance that too tools, such as Quality Audits, Quality Control and specifically System Audits that the processes tools, and safeguards are in place to produce quality products.

Quality Audit: An independent investigation and assessment of quality activities and results to determine whether or not the quality plan is effective and appropriate.

Quality Control (QC): The use of techniques and activities that compare about quality performance with goals and define appropriate action in response to a short fall.

Quality Improvement (QI): A systematic approach to the processes of work that looks to remove waste, loss, rework, frustration etc., to make the work more effective, efficient and appropriate.

Total Quality Management (TQM): Management approach of an organization centres on quality based on the participation of all its members and aiming at long term success through customer satisfaction and benefits to all members of the organization and to society.

Managing for quality in all aspects of an organization focusing on employee participation and customer satisfaction is TQM.

Continuous (Quality) Improvement (C.I. or CQI): Ongoing improvement of any kind and all aspects of an organization including its products, services, communications, environment, functions, individual process etc.

Continuous Improvement Action taken to find ways to improve processes, decrease variation, decrease costs, and improve effectiveness of the organization.

CQI is a global approach to business development that establishes an integrated program through, which a company can achieve continuously incremented improvements in its chosen key performance measures by focusing on the better leadership of people and the improved management of business processes.

Total Quality Management (TQM)

Came into being in 80's because of intense competition Technology-
-Establishes strong link with HRD function

Quality Engineering   -Customer focused

-Employee oriented

Systematic approach to implement lasting changes in an organization through the use of:

    a. Teamwork and participation

    b. Statistical methods and analyses

    c. Management leadership

    d. Problem solving and process management

Quality In Healthcare

Road towards TQM (Total Quality Management)

⬇
Decide

⬇
Prepare

⬇
Start

⬇
Expand

⬇
Integrate

⬇

TQM – Process (Juran's Triology)

Quality Planning

Quality Control

Quality Improvement

[Design for Quality]

TQM is an approach for continuously improving the quality goods and services, delivered through the participation of all levels and functions of the organization.

Total Quality Management - Steps

Customer's Focus

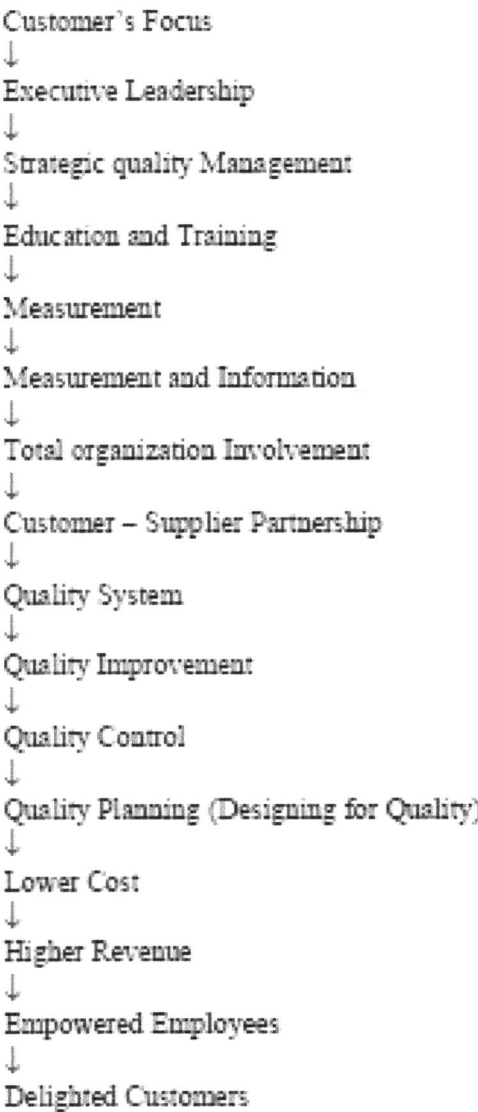

Customer's Focus
↓
Executive Leadership
↓
Strategic quality Management
↓
Education and Training
↓
Measurement
↓
Measurement and Information
↓
Total organization Involvement
↓
Customer – Supplier Partnership
↓
Quality System
↓
Quality Improvement
↓
Quality Control
↓
Quality Planning (Designing for Quality)
↓
Lower Cost
↓
Higher Revenue
↓
Empowered Employees
↓
Delighted Customers

Continuous Quality Improvement (CQI)

CQI uses quality management practices to obtain top quality performance management techniques are allied to a process- designed to make sure the company does not stand in the way of the staff delivering a top performance.

The core of the program is the business survival strategy.

1. Determine the functions that need to be done.
2. Ensure the right processes are used in the right functions.
3. Get the right people to do the right jobs.
4. Have the products, services, processes and procedures that are customer focused for both external and internal customers.
5. When implementing the program, one should remember that processes are rational with predictable outcomes, whereas people are so complex that their responses can be non-rational and cannot be accurately predicted).

Continuous Quality Improvement

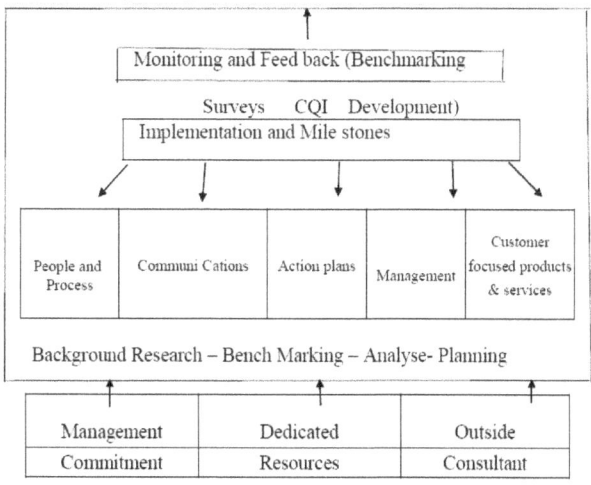

Background Research – Bench Marking – Analyse- Planning

Quality Gurus

To understand the modern quality movement, it is necessary to understand the philosophic of notable individuals, who have shaped the evolution of quality. Their philosophic and teachings have contributed to our knowledge and understanding of quality. They are often referred to as Quality Gurus.

Walter A. Schewart : He was born in 1891 in U.S.A. He studied Physics, Engineering and Statistics. He was a statistician at Bell Labs during 1920's and 1930's. Schewart studied randomness and recognized that variability existed in all manufacturing processes. He developed quality control charts that are used to identify whether variability in the process is random or due to an assignable cause, such as poor workers or mis calibrated machinery. He stressed that eliminating variability improves quality.

Schewart identified two categories of variation.

- Assignable cause or special cause
- Chance cause or common cause variation. He devised the control chart as a tool for distinguishing between the two.

Schewart reported that bringing a process into a state of statistical control, where there is only chance cause (common cause) variation and in keeping it in control was needed to reduce waste and improve quality. His work created the foundation for today's Statistical Process Control and he is often referred to as the 'Grandfather of Quality Control'

Edwards Deming: He was born in 1900 in the U.S. He was an engineer, mathematician, physicist and statistician. After World War II he assisted many Japanese companies in improving quality.

A number of elements of Deming's philosophy depend from traditional notions of quality. The first is the role of management should play in a company's quality improvement effort. Historically, poor quality was blamed on workers – on their lack of productivity, laziness or carelessness. However, Deming pointed out that only 15% of quality problems are actually due to worker errors. The remaining 85% are caused by processes and systems, including poor management. Deming said that it was up to the management to correct system problems and create an environment that promotes quality and enables workers to achieve their full potential.

He believed that managers should drive out any fear employees have of identifying quality problems and that numerical quotes should be eliminated. Proper methods should be taught and detecting and eliminating poor quality should be the responsibility of all.

Deming outlines his philosophy in his famous 14 points – it has three basic percepts:

- Customer Orientation
- Continuous Improvement
- Quality is determined by the system

Deming's Absolutes of Quality

- Do it right first time
- Defects prevention is the only acceptable approach

Deming's deadly sins of Western Management

- Lack of constancy of purpose to plan product and services that will have a market, keep the company in business and enable it provide jobs.
- Emphasis on short-term profit thinking, fed by fear of turnover push from bankers.

Deming's fourteen points.

1. Create constancy of purpose for product/ service quality.
2. Allocate resources for long range needs rather than short term profitability.
3. Adopt the New Philosophy No longer to live with commonly accepted levels of delays, mistakes, defective materials and defective workmanship.
4. Cease Dependence upon mass inspection.
5. End "Lowest Tender" contracts (single reliable supplier)
6. Improve every process
7. Institute training on the Job
8. Adopt and institute leadership

9. Drive out fear Encourage effective two-way communication and other means to drive out fear throughout the organization.
10. Break down Barriers Between staff areas and departments
11. Eliminate slogans, exhortations and targets to the work force.
12. Demanding zero defects and new levels of productivity without providing method
13. Eliminate Arbitrary Numerical Targets
14. Permit pride of workmanship
15. Encourage education
16. Vigorous program of education Encourage self-improvement for everyone
17. Take action to accomplish the transformation. Top management's commitment for that.

Joseph Juran – He was born in 1904. He was an engineer. He is considered to have the greatest impact on quality management. Juran originally worked in quality program of Western Electric. Though his philosophy is similar to Deming's, there are some differences. Deming stressed the need for organizational transformation. Juran suggested that quality management should be embedded in the organization.

Juran defined quality as "Fitness for Use" rather than simply conformance to specifications to specifications. He is also credited with developing the concept of cost of quality, which allows to measure quality in financial terms, rather than on the basis of subjective evaluations.

Juran is well known for originating the idea of quality trilogy.

➢ Quality Planning: To identify their customer's product requirements and overriding business goals. Processes should be set up to ensure that quality standards are met.

➢ Quality Control: Stresses the regular use of statistical control methods to ensure that quality standards are met and to identify

➢ variations from the standards.

➢ Quality Improvement: It should be continuous as well as breakthrough. To implement continuous improvement, workers need to have training in proper methods on a regular basis.

Juran's ten steps to Quality Improvement.

- Build awareness of the need and opportunity for improvement.
- Set goals for improvement
- Organize to reach the goals
- (Establish a quality council, Identify problems, Select
- projects, Appoint teams, Designate facilitators)
- Provide Training
- Carry out projects to solve problems
- Report Progress
- Give Recognition
- Communicate results
- Keep score

Philip Crosby: He was born in 1936. He worked in the area of quality for many years. He developed a phrase **"Do it right the first time"** and the notion **"Zero Defect"** – arguing that no number of defects should be acceptable. He served the idea that a small number of defects is normal part of the operating process because systems and workers are imperfect. Instead, he stressed the idea of prevention. He is also famous for coining the phrase **"Quality is Free"**. According to him, many costs of quality which include not only the costs of wasted labour equipment time, scrap, rework and lost sales but also organizational costs that are hard to quantify. Crosby stressed that efforts to improve quality more than pay for themselves because costs are prevented. Therefore, quality is free.

Like Deming and Juran, Crossby stressed the role of management in the quality improvement effort and the use of statistical control tools, in measuring and monitoring quality.

- Management Commitment
- The Quality Improvement Team
- Quality Measurement
- To display current and potential non-conformance problems
- to permit Objective evaluation and corrective action.
- The Cost of Quality

- To define the ingredients of the cost of quality and explain its use as a management tool.
- Quality Awareness By all persons
- Corrective action
- Systemic method of resolving the problems.
- Zero Defects Planning (not close to)
- Supervisor Training
- Realization of Change By all the employees
- Goal setting
- To establish improvement goals by all individuals.
- Error-Cause Removal Problems Faced by the employees
- Recognition To appreciate those who participate.
- Quality Councils To bring together the professional quality people for planned communication on regular basis.
- Do It Over again
- To emphasize that the quality improvement program never ends.

Kaoru Ishikawa: He was born in 1915 in Japan and worked as professor in a university. He is best known for the development of quality tools called "Cause and Effect" diagram also known as Fishbone and Ishikawa diagrams. These diagrams are used for quality problem solving. He was the first quality guru to emphasize the importance of the internal customer, the next person in the production process. He was also one of the first to stress the importance of total company quality control, rather than just focusing on products and services.

Dr. Ishikawa believed that everyone in the company needed to be united with a shared vision and a common goal. He stressed that quality initiatives should be pursued at every level of the organization and that all employees should be involved.

Dr. Ishikawa was a proponent of implementation of quality circles. He advocated user friendly quality control

- One step further
- Companywide quality control

- Continued customer services once the product is sold.
- Reliance on consumer need

Genichi Taguchi – was born in 1924. He was an engineer and statistician. He was a quality expert known for his work in the area of product design. He estimated that almost 80% of all defective items are caused by poor product design. He stressed that the companies should focus their quality efforts on the design stage as it was much cheaper and easier to make changes during the product design stage than during the production process.

Taguchi is known for applying a concept called 'design of experiment' to product design. His philosophy is based on the idea that it is easier to design a product that can perform over a wide range of environmental conditions.

Taguchi had a large impact on today's view of costs of conformance to specifications.

- Taguchi less function used to measure financial loss to society resulting from poor quality.
- The philosophy of off line quality control designing products and process so that they are to parameters outside designer engineer's control.
- Innovations in the statistical design of experiments notably the use of an outer array of factors that are uncontrollable in real life but are systematically varied in the experiment.
- **Shigio Shingo** - Born in 1909. He was an Industrial Engineer. He was one of the leading experts on manufacturing practices and the Toyota Production System.
- His main contributions include Poka – Yoke (A miske-proofing mechanism) Single Minute Exchange of Dues (SMED) Just in Time (JIT)

Yoshio Kondo - was born in 1910. He was a biologist. His biggest contribution is his emphasis on the interrelationship between quality and people. He sees humanity as the essence of motivation. He endorses that human work should always include the following components

- Creativity – the joy of thinking

- Physical Activity – The joy of working with sweat on the forehead.
- Socially, the joy of sharing pleasure and pain with colleagues.
- He suggests four points of action in support of such process.
- When giving work instruction, clarify the true aims of the work.
- See that people have a strong sense of responsibility towards their work
- Give time for the creation of ideas
- Nurture ideas and bring them for function.
- These are some of the great quality Gurus. Since then and earlier, have contributed to development of quality. In fact, it is a continuous process ever changing and every getting modified.

Quality Management System

Quality Management system (QMS) is a set of coordinated activities to direct and control an organization in order to continually improve the effectiveness and efficiency of its performance.

It is also the procedures explicitly designed to monitor assess and improve the quality of care.

The main thrust of Quality Management System is defining the processes which will result in the production of quality products and service rather than in detecting defective products or services after they have been produced.

A fully documented QMS will ensure that two important requirements are met

a) Customer requirements: Confidence is the ability of the organization to deliver the desired product and service consistently meeting their needs and expectations.

b) The organization's requirements both internally and externally and at the optimum cost with efficient use of the available resources like materials, humans, technology and information.

These requirements can be met if objective evidence is provided in the form of information and data to support the system activities from the ultimate supplier to the ultimate customer.

The QMS enables an organization to achieve the goals and objectives, set out its policy and strategy. It provides consistency and satisfaction in terms of methods, materials, environment, etc. and interacts with all activities of the organization beginning with the identification of customer requirements and ending with their satisfaction at every transaction interface.

Management Systems are needed in all activities of activity; whether large or small business manufacturing service or public sector.

A good QMS should:

- Set directions
- Must meet customers' expectations

- Improve process control
- Reduce wastage
- Lower costs
- Increase market share
- Facilitate training
- Involve staff
- Raise morale

Setting up of a QMS

- Adoption of QMS needs to be a strategic decision of an organization. It is influenced by
- Varying needs, Objectives
- The products/services provided
- The size and structure of the organization
- QMS must ensure that the products and services confirm to customer needs and expectations and the objectives of the organizations.
- Issues to be considered when setting up QMS
- Design
- Built
- Control
- Deployment
- Measurement
- Review
- Improvement

Design and Build – include the structure of quality management system the process and its implementation. Its design must ideally be led by senior managers to suit the needs of the organization. Design of the QMS should come from determining the organizations core processes and well-defined goals and strategies and be linked to the needs of one or more stakeholders.

The process of designing and building the QMS must also be clear with the quality function playing a key role but involvement and buy-in to the system must also come from all other functions.

- Deployment and Implementation is best achieved using process packages where each core process is broken down into sub-process and described by a combination of documentation, education training, tools systems and metrics

- Control of the QMS – depends on the size and complexity of the organization. Local control where possible is effective and good practice is found where key stakeholders are documented within the process and where the process owner is allowed to control all the processes. Ideally, process owners/operators are involved in writing procedures.

- Measurement is to determine the effectiveness and efficiency of each process towards attiring its objectives. It should include the contribution of the QMS to the organization's goals. This could be achieved by measuring the following

➢ Policy definition and completeness

➢ Coverage of business

➢ Reflection of policies

➢ Deployment

➢ Usage

➢ Whether staffs find the QMS helpful in their work

➢ Speed of change of the QMS

➢ Relevance of QMS architecture to the job in need

A form of scorecard deployed through the organization down to individual objective level can be employed and the setting of targets at all levels is vital.

Review of the effectiveness and capability of a QMS is vital and the outcome of these employees. Reviewing and monitoring should be conducted, whether or not improvement activities have achieved the expected outcomes.

> Improvement should be as a result of the review process, with the aim of seeking internal best practice. It is part of the overall improvement activities and an integration of managing within the organization.

There are eight brand principles upon which to base an efficient effective and adaptable QMS. They are applicable throughout industry, commerce and the service sectors.

> Customer focus
> Leadership
> Involving People
> Process Approach
> System's Approach
> Continual Improvement
> Factual Decision making
> Mutually beneficial supplier relationships

Customer Focus – Customer needs and expectations must be determined and converted into product requirements.

Leadership – To be done by providing unity of purpose through an appropriate quality policy, ensuring that measurable objectives are established and demonstratively they are fully committed to developing, sustaining and improving the QMS.

Involvement of people – at levels of the organization is essential. This includes ensuring that there is an awareness of the importance of meeting customer requirements and responsibilities in doing this and people are competent on the basis of appropriate training and experience.

Process Approach: Must be at its core. Each process must transform one or more inputs to create an output of value to the customer.

The core business processes, should define the activities that directly add value to the product or service for the external customer and support the processes that are required to maintain the effectiveness of the core process.

Systems Approach: The processes must be thoroughly understood and managed, so that the most efficient use is made of available resources to ensure that the needs of all the stakeholders, customers, employees, shareholders and the community are met.

Continual Improvement - To achieve this attention needs to be given to both the voices of the customer through complaint analysis, opinion surveys and regular contacts through measurement, monitoring and analysis of both process and product data. Mutually Beneficial Supplier Relationships for long term needs of the organization they are necessary.

A good QMS will not function or improve without adequate audits and reviews.

Audits: are carried out to ensure that actual methods are adhering to the documented procedures while system reviews should be carried out periodically and systematically to ensure the system achieves the required effect.

There should be scheme for carrying out audits with different activities possibly requiring different frequencies. Audits should indicate, the necessary improvement and corrective actions but must also determine if processes are effective and that responsibilities have been correctly assigned.

The emphasis on process improvement and enhancing customer satisfaction, requires a more thoughtful approach to auditing.

The generic steps involved are

- **Initiation:** Scope and Frequency
- **Preparation:** Review of documentation, the program
- working documents.
- **Execution:** Opening meeting, Examinations and Evaluation, Collecting Evidence, Observations, Close the meeting with the auditors.
- **Report:** Preparation, content, distribution
- **Completion:** Report Submission, Retention

Quality Management System Review

It should take place, possibly once a year. It should cover

- Results of audits

- Customer Feedback
- Process and Product conformity
- Follow up actions from previous management reviews.
- Change that could affect the QMS
- Recommendations for improvements

Plan – Do – Check – Act (PDCA) Cycle

Plan-Do-Check-Act cycle is a basic principle on which most QMS are based. It is a checklist of the four stages, which an organization must go through to get from 'problem-faced' to 'problem solved'.

We cannot talk about Continuous Quality Improvement without mentioning two of its founding fathers, Walker Shewhart and W. Edwards Deming. Shewhart created a scientific method for process improvement. His model was described in the three-step process of specification, production, and inspection. Later, Deming advanced this model into what we know today as Plan, Do, Check (Study), Act, or PDSA. We use the PDSA Model as an effective tool to solve problems within an organization.

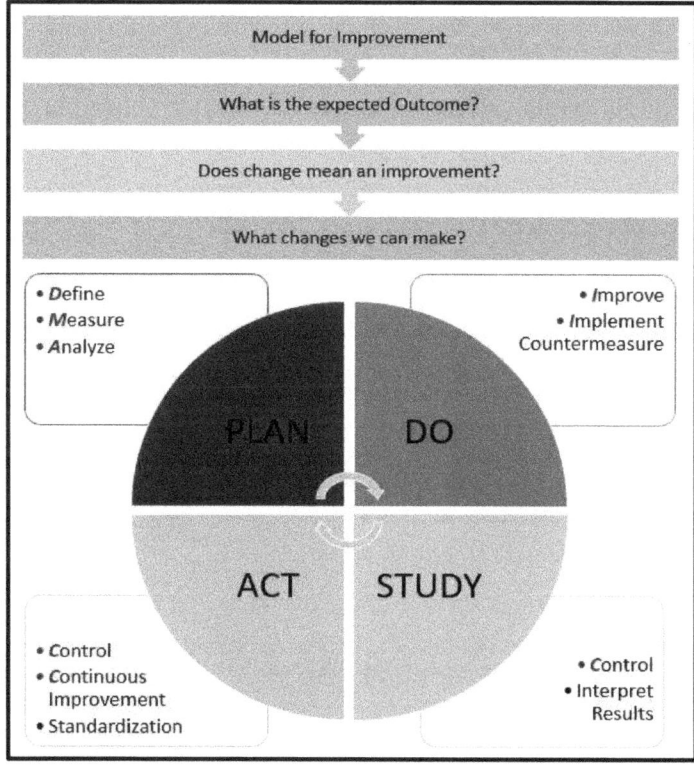

[Source: *Office of Assessment, Accreditation and Continuous Quality Improvement, Wayne State University School of Medicine, Michigan.*]

The concept of PDCA cycle was originally developed by Walter Schewart. It was taken up and promoted very effectively in 1950's by Edwards, Deming. Consequently, known as Deming's Wheel or Cycle.

Plan Step 1: Identify the Problem

- Select the problem to be analysed
- Clearly define the problem and establish a precise problem
- Statement
- Set a measurable goal for the problem-solving effort.
- Establish a process for coordinating with and gaining
- Approval of leadership.

Plan Step 2: Analyse the Problem

- Identify the processes that impact the problem and select one.
- List the steps in the process as it currently exists.
- Map the Process.
- Validate the map of the process
- Identify potential cause of the problem
- Collect and analyse data related to the problem.
- Verify root causes of the problem
- Collect additional data if needed to verify root causes.

Do Step 3: Develop Solutions

- Establish criteria for selecting a solution
- Generate potential solutions that will address the root causes
- of the problem
- Select a solution
- Gain approval and supporters for the chosen solution

- Plan the solution

Do Step 4: Implement a Solution
- Implement the chosen solution on a trial or pilot basis. This minimizes disruption to routine activity while testing whether the changes will work or not.

Check Step 5: Evaluate the Results
- Gather data on the solution
- Analyse the data on the solution
- Check whether the small scale or experimental changes are achieving the desired result or not.
- Also, continuously check nominated key activities (regardless of any experimentation going on) to ensure that you know what the quality of the output is at all times to identify any new problems when they crop up.

Achieved the Desired Goal? If YES, go to Step 6. If NO, go back to Step 1

Act Step 6: Standardize the solution (and Capitalize on New Opportunities)
- Identify systemic changes and training needs for full implementation.
- Adopt the solution
- Plan ongoing monitoring of the solution
- Continue to look for incremental improvements to refine the solution
- Look for another improvement opportunity

PDCA describes the overall stages of improvement activity, but how is each stage carried out? This is where other specific quality management or continuous improvement, tools and techniques come into play

Kaoru Ishikawa: has expanded Deming's four steps into Six

- Determine goals and targets
- Determine methods of reaching goals
- Engage in Education and training Implement work
- Check the effects of implementation
- Take appropriate action

Deming's PDCA Cycle (Plan-Do-Check-Act)

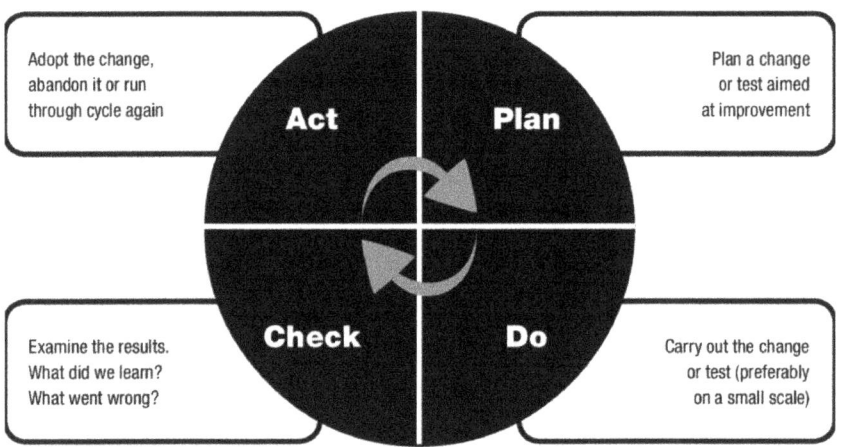

Paradigm Shift - In Last Few Decades

Old Belief	New Paradigm
Managing a job	Managing is through leadership and is a way of life (It requires one to reduce the size of one's ego and to increase the importance of all others in one's mind).
Concept of external customer alone	Concept of external and internal customers.
Marketing assignment is to sell what is being produced	Organizations must accurately assess the customer's needs and then go about satisfying them.
Workers are just hand and feet. They have to be told what to do.	The potential in each human being is enormous and is just waiting to be used. The feelings and brains of each person are more important and not his hand and feet.
People don't like to work or produce good quality and will always do as little as possible unless they have strong supervision or incentives.	People enjoy working and produce good quality if they are trained properly, are given responsibility and authority to make change at their work place and are treated with respect (Concept of TEI)
Quality is headache of Quality Control.	Quality of everybody's responsibility and principally of producers (Concept of TQC).
Good house-keeping is nice but not important	Top quality cannot be produced without excellent house-keeping (Concept of 5S)

A reasonable inventory of raw materials and in-process materials is essential to avoid production stoppages.	The lower the sustainable level of inventory the more efficient is the production process-the target of inventory being zero (Concept of JIT).
Economic batch quality quantity is calculated from set up time and inventory carrying cost. Generally speaking, production is best served by large batch size.	Target is batch size of one. Set up time is to be made insignificant.
Suppliers are necessary evils and should never be trusted.	Choose a supplier and build a long-term trust relationship.
Once sold, the product is forgotten. No attention is paid to after sales service.	Service manuals, spare parts, service technology are all managed systematically.
Crisis management. Problems are dealt with as they crop up with no understanding of why they do so.	PDCA wheel is conscientiously rotated. People are not afraid to reveal weaknesses and take responsibility for their work.

In the recent years another Paradigm shift has been taking place because of IT revolution. There is increased focus on automation, teamwork and process to get better quality products and services.

Japanese Management

Rapid progress made by Japan in providing quality products at competitive prices attracted the whole world. Many countries adopted these methods sometimes with modifications. Common features are as follows.

Disciplined workers. Give maximum importance to their jobs and take their jobs very seriously. Sense of responsibility (the next worker need not check the machines because he is certain that previous worker has done it). Experts in planning, Scheduling, conducting in time.

After 2nd World War they learnt lessons of quality rather painfully which they still continue to practice. Passion for excellence. Work harder and longer on their own. Life time employment. Good industrial relations. Synergy in whole system. Concepts of Total Quality Management imbibed in entire system. Concepts like JIT. Integrated Supplier-Customer relationship. Statistical analysis. Full support from the management for quality programs. Actively practice Kai Zen – continuous improvement. Continuously educate and train the employees (at least 22 days in a year). Excellent management. Facilities. Responsible employees. Little or no inventories. Absence of work stoppages. Almost no rejected products. Absence of Crisis management and excellent maintenance of equipment. Technological advantages because of insistence on building their process in house. Skilled employees trained in-house. Effective integration of operations policy and manufacturing strategy. They focus on long-term objectives and not on short cuts and small gains. Workers belong to company unions rather than craft unions. Practice the concept of consensus decision-making. Collective responsibility and team rewards. Socialization of Japanese Firm to inculcate the culture of the organization in the employees by such rituals as singing company songs. After hours group activities. Company sponsored vacations. Develop and sustain long term commitment and loyalty to organization. Directors are from Company (not form outside) they rise in the company. Dividends on the share values (not on market value). A large part of profit is pumped back into the company to improve the techniques management etc.

Though the current Japanese management is broadly based on the above methods and philosophy it has undergone changes. Adopting good practices from other countries and adopting to the needs of changing technology.

American Management

It has its own methods and philosophy.

It can be described as individualistic in approach in so far as managers are accountable for the decisions made within their areas of responsibility. Although important decisions might be discussed in an open forum, the ultimate responsibility for the consequences of the decisions lies with the boss. The positive aspect of this accountability is that outstanding success – will bring outstanding rewards. The American managers are more likely to disregard the opinions of subordinates which may lead to frustrations of the latter.

Comparison between American and Japanese Managements

Both the styles are different, and it is not easy to decide which is better, because both are successful models. American companies seem to be excellent in their management style because, they are able to survive for a long time they make more profit and they grow faster than companies in other countries. But Japanese management is considered more efficient.

Japanese management is a great example when it comes to job security and health areas. Japanese organizations follow the beliefs that an individual should be contributing to the society as a whole. On the other hand, American companies are focused more on satisfying themselves first and only then comes the society.

In Japanese management companies people are a lot more important than money or anything else. Managers and their employees can be viewed as a big family where each of them takes care of another. There a minimum unit is an individual, while in an American corporation, the minimum unit is represented by a job. American Employers focus on preparing the right job descriptions first and then they try to find the right person with the right skills and abilities tome the requirements needed for a successful performance of that job. But the Japanese employers believe that each person has his/her, own skills that will show what kind of job is suitable for that particular person. So, there is no need to advertise the job description beforehand.

Employers will just assign the right jobs to the new employees, after learning about their abilities.

Japanese managers and their employees act like a big family they feel a great loyalty towards the company they work for. Even the contracts are based on trust between employers and their employees, while in America the contracts are based on concrete, job descriptions and other details. Moreover, the great loyalty of Japanese workers also accrues, from the fact that companies guarantee their employees a very good job security until they reach the age of 60 years whereas most of the American companies do not guarantee anything when it comes to a job security. Furthermore, while layoffs are very common and often in America, in Japan such actions are highly unacceptable in the society. Layoffs in Japan occur only if an emergency comes up such as bad employees, discipline or bankruptcy.

When hiring a new employee, Japanese companies look for someone, who is cheerful, active, eager and willing to devote himself / herself to the company, so they often do not hire employees based on their skills and knowledge. On the contrary American companies specifically hire only those who are suitable for the particular job based on their abilities and proper education. The responsibility for a project in Japanese companies is given to a whole team than just one person like it is in American companies, where a team leader is usually the only one responsible for the project.

The managers in Japanese organizations are responsible for their employees and that they care for them. The managers emphasize the importance of good relationships with their subordinates because it seems to ensure good work performances and better deals. Even though Japanese Managers prefer and support harmony and equity, between team members. They also support criticizing among themselves. All compliments or criticism are directed to the whole team. On the contrary Americans do not use direct criticizing and they pay almost no attentions to group harmony. All punishments or rewards in American corporations depend on individual performances of employees.

QUALITY TOOLS

Quality tools are used for various purposes related to controlling and assuming quality. A large number of quality tools, specific to certain domains, fields and practices are available. They can be organized into six categories.

Quality In Healthcare

Seven Basic tools of Quality: It is a designation given to a fixed set of graphical techniques identified as being most helpful in troubleshooting issues. They are called basic because they are suitable for people with little formal training in statistics and because they can be used to solve the vast majority of quality related issues. Proper usage of these seven basic quality tools is the first step towards successful process improvements.

1. Flow Chart
2. Cause and Effect Diagram
3. Pareto Chart
4. Check Shot
5. Control Chart
6. Histogram
7. Scatter Diagram

The first four are used primarily to help understand the process to identify potential causes for process performance, problems and to collect and display data indicating, which are most prevalent. The last three are used for more precise data analysis.

Flow Chart (Process Flowchart, Process Flow Diagram, Run Chart)

A flow chart is a picture of the separate steps of a process in sequential order. The process described can by anything a manufacturing process, an administrative or service process, or a project plan.

Generally appropriate symbols are used to prepare the flow chart Symbols for Flow Charts

- Start or stop
- Document
- Decision
- Delay

Flowchart is used to develop the understanding of a process is done and to communicate to others about the process. It is used to modify and change the process for better results.

Cause and Effect Diagram

They are charts that identify potential causes for particular quality problems.

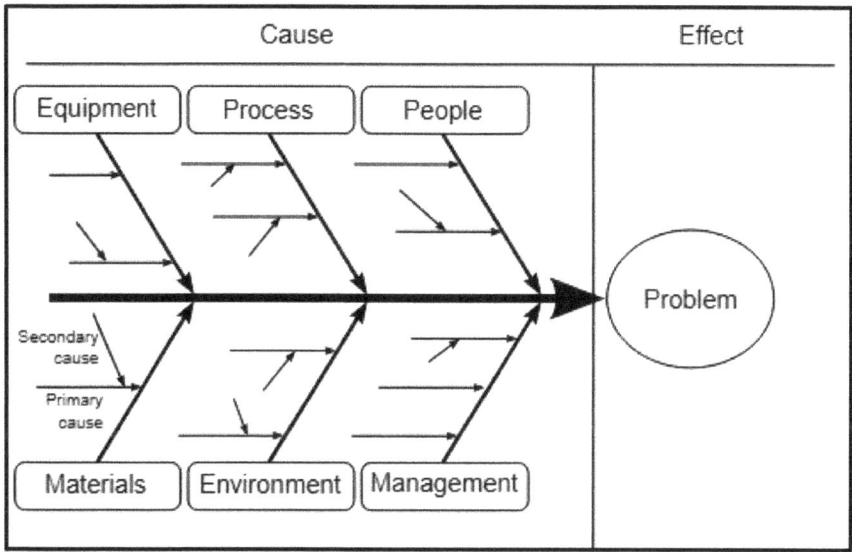

The 'head' of the fish is the quality problem, such as damaged zippers on a garment or broken valves on a tire. The diagram is drawn so that the spine of the fish connects the head to the possible cause of the problem. These causes could be related to the machines, workers, measurement, suppliers, materials and many other aspects of production process. Each of these possible causes can then have smaller bones that address specific issues that relate to each cause. For example, these possible causes can then smaller bones that address specific issues that relate to each cause. For example, a problem with machines could be due to a need for adjustment, old equipment or tooling problems. Similarly, a problem with workers could be related to lack of training, poor supervision or fatigue.

Cause and effect diagrams are problem solving tools, commonly used by quality control teams, where specific causes of problems can be explored through brainstorming the development of a cause and effects – diagram requires the team to think through all possible causes of poor quality.

Pareto Chart (Pareto diagram, Pareto Analysis 80/20 Rule)

The Pareto Chart, named after Italian Economist Vilfredo Pareto. It is a technique used to identify quality problems, based on their degree of importance. The logic behind Pareto Chart is that only a few quality problems are important whereas many others are not critical. In quality management the logic behind Pareto principle is that most quality problems are a result of only a few causes. The trick is to identify these causes.

To use Pareto analysis, a chart should be developed that ranks the causes of poor quality in decreasing order based on the percentage of defects each has caused. For example, a tally can be made of the number of defects that result from different causes, such as operator error, defective parts, or inaccurate machine calibrations. Percentage of defects can be computed from the tally

Pareto Chart

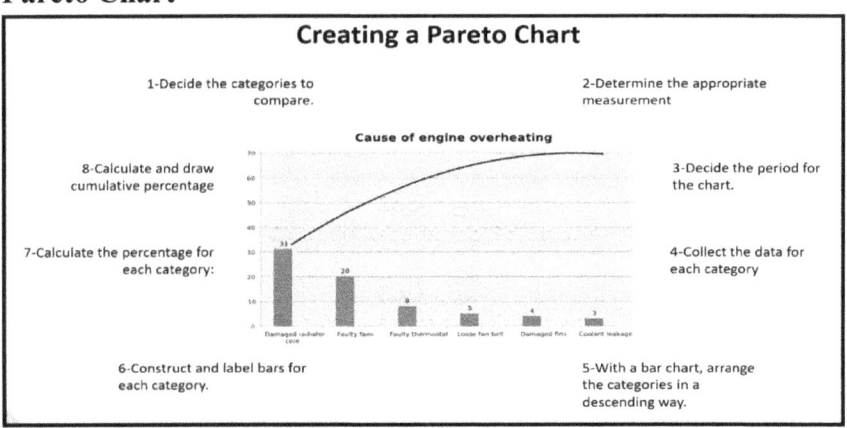

Some of the conclusions drawn based on Pareto Principle are

- 80% of the quality costs came from 20% of the problems.
- 80% of the sales go to 20% of the customers
- 80% of the performance of the people comes from 20% of their
- activities
- 85% of the problems are caused by management and 15% are caused by subordinates.

Check sheet – (Check List)

It is a list of common defects and the number of observed occurrences of those defects. It is a simple yet effective fact-finding tool that allows the worker to collect specific information regarding the defects observed.

A Check Sheet refers to a document used for recording data at the time and place of the operation of interest. Typically, a blank document is taken to start with. Then it is designed for easy, quick, and effective recording of the required data, which can be either qualitative or quantitative.

This sheet helps identify all possible errors and has the flexibility to add more sources of error based on practical experience. These are then used for recording data about the errors, which are eventually used for analyzing the operational issue. This sheet is an important part of Dr. Kaoru Ishikawa's seven quality control tools.

CHECK SHEET - DAILY REJECTION MONITORING

PART NAME: PART NO.:   MODEL:

S. NO.	DEFECT	\multicolumn{7}{c}{Date wise Rejection}	Total
		1	2	3	4	5	6	7	
1	Blow Hole	15	12	10	13	11	8	10	79
2	Non filling	5	10	8	2	5	6	4	40
3	Catching	8	5	8	5	7	9	6	48
4	Carbon	12	11	8	6	4	8	9	58
5	Crack	9	13	10	8	11	5	7	63
	Total	49	51	44	34	38	36	36	

Checklist

It shows four defects and the number of times, they have been observed. It is clear that the biggest problem is ripped material. This means that the plant needs to focus on this focus problem. For example, by going to the source of supply or seeing whether the material rips during a particular production process. A check list can also be used to focus on other dimensions, such as location or time. For example, if a defect is being observed frequently a checklist can be developed, that measure the number of occurrences per shift, per machine or per operator. In this fashion, one can isolate the location of the particular defect and then focus correcting the problem.

Control Chart

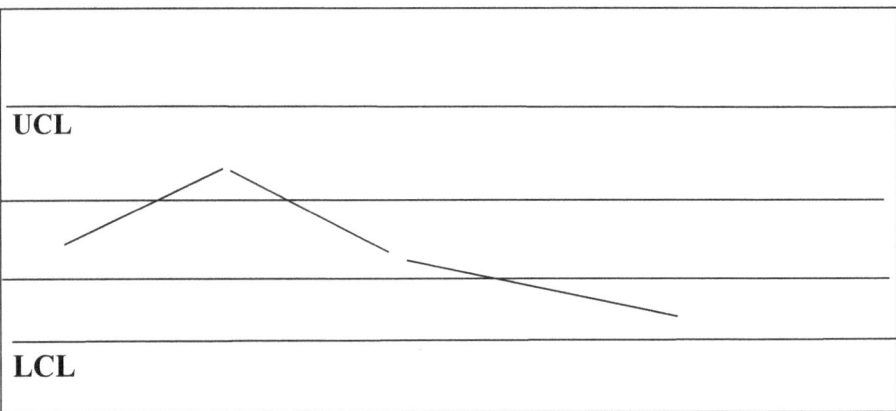

These charts are used to evaluate whether a process is operating within expectations, relative to some measured value such as weight, width or volume. For example, one could measure the weight of sack of floor, the width of a tire, or the volume of a bottle of soft drink. When the production process is operating within expectations, it is termed "In Control".

To evaluate, whether or not a process is in control one needs to regularly measure the variable of interest and plot it on a control chart.

The chart has a line down the center representing the arrange value of the variable one is measuring. Above and below the center lines called the upper control limit (UCL) and the lower control limit (LCL). As long as the observed values within the upper and lower control limits, the process is in control and there is no problem with the quality. When a measured observation falls outside these limits, there is a problem.

Histogram

It is a chart which shows the frequency distribution of observed values of a variable. One can see from the plot what type of distribution a particular valuable displays. Such as whether it has a normal distribution and whether the distribution is symmetrical.

Quality In Healthcare

Frequency

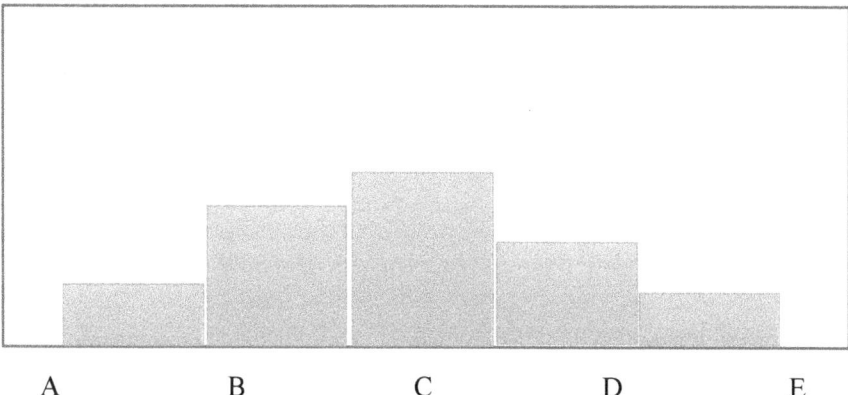

A   B   C   D   E

- They are used to display and identify the type of distribution of data by drawing graphs for the number of units in each class of the data.

- Histograms show different shape and can indicate a probable cause for the deviation from most frequent shape (normal shape).

- Different shapes of histogram, provide an insight into the value of the data.

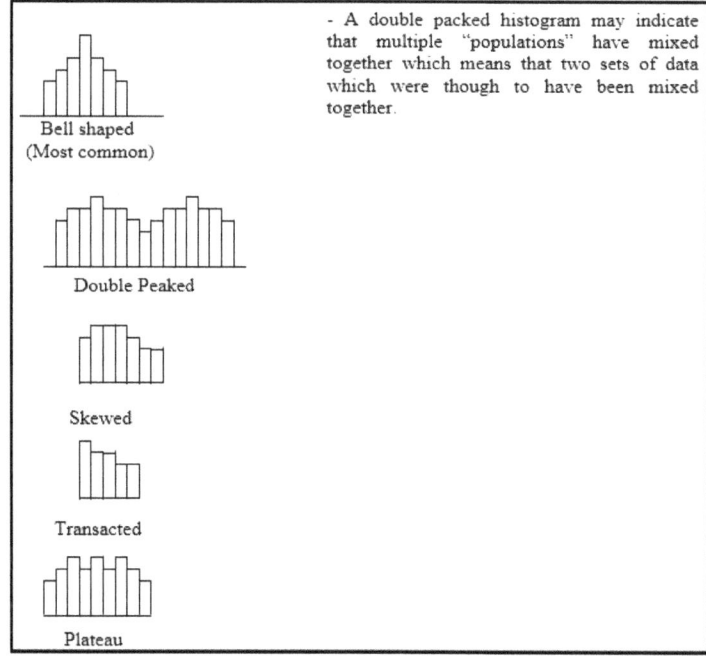

Histograms can indicate the reasons, why process are incapable of holding the required tolerances.

SCATTER DIAGRAMS

They are graphs that show how two variables are related to another. They are particularly useful in detecting the amount of correlation or the degree of linear relationship between two variables.

A scatter diagram is used to examine the relationship between both the axes (X and Y) with one variable. In the graph, if the variables are correlated, then the point drops along a curve or line. A scatter diagram or scatter plot gives an idea of the nature of relationship.

In a scatter correlation diagram, if all the points stretch in one line, then the correlation is perfect and is in unity. However, if the scatter points are widely scattered throughout the line, then the correlation is said to be low. If the scatter points rest near a line or on a line, then the correlation is said to be linear.

For example, increased production speed and number of defects. Two variables could also be correlated negatively, so that an increase in one of the variables is associated with a decrease in the other. For example, increased worker training might be associated with a decrease in the number of defects observed.

The greater the degree of correlation, the more linear are the observations in the diagram, the less correlation exists between the variables, other types of relationships can also be observed on a scatter diagram..

This may be the case when one is observing the relationship between two variables such as even temperature and number of defects. Since temperatures below and above the ideal could lead to defects.

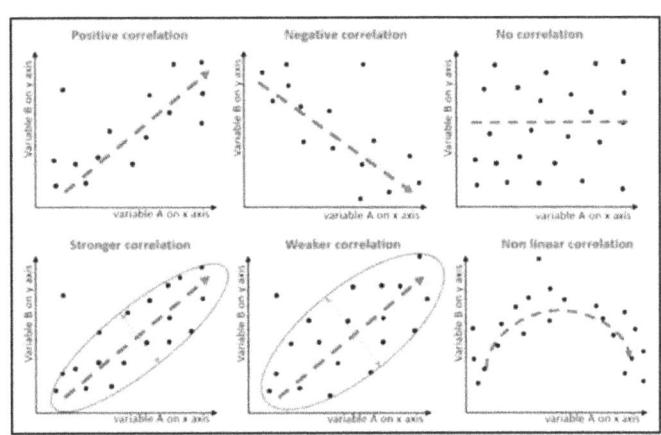

Seven Management Tools
Listed in order that moves from abstract analysis to detailed planning.

1. Affinity diagram
2. Interrelationship diagram
3. Tree diagram
4. Matrix diagram
5. Matrix data analysis / priority
6. Arrow diagrams / activity network diagram
7. Process decision / program chart (PDPC)

These tools are used to analyse conceptual and qualitatively oriented information, such as that prevalent while planning organizational change or project management.

The Affinity Diagram (K-J Method)
It is a group brainstorming and organizing technique.

Team members begin by brainstorming freely on a defined topic. Ideas are written on individual cards or adhesive note papers and arrayed on a surface for everyone to see. After a period of brainstorming, the team then shifts all its attention to grouping the ideas into sensible categories. In silence each team member searches for two cards that he or she feels are related in some way. These cards are then placed together, and the process is repeated continuously with team members finding two new cards that are related or adding additional cards to existing groups. In this process cards are said to have an "affinity" or attraction for one another because the individual ideas on them see related in some way. The silent grouping continues until all cards have been placed into six to ten groups. At this point the team switches from silent work to discussion mode examining each group identify the central theme that ties them all together.

This theme is written on header card with the individual items arranged under it, to complete the diagram. The brainstorming allows everyone to participate freely, while the silent grouping allows new patterns of information to emerge by postponing the critical thinking that tends to push information into the mould of preconceived patterns. Finally, the process of naming the group establishes a common understanding among team members as to the central themes reflected in the collection of ideas.

A relations diagram (also known as interrelationships diagram) Documents complex cause – effect relationships among items. The construction of the diagram is participatory and verbal. Items are written on individual cards and displayed on a wall or easel sheet. These items might be the themes (header cards) from an earlier affinity diagram considering one card at a time the leader asks the team. Which other items are driven by or influenced by the factor.

Process Decision Program Chart (PDPC)

It maps out conceivable but undesirable events in a plan and indicates appropriate contingencies.

Planning teams typically construct POPC's near the end of their planning efforts. Utilizing the collective knowledge of the team to perform a final check of an implementation plan. The team begins as with a tree diagram by defining a goal (level 1) and the high-level steps that contribute to the goal (level 2). Then instead of breaking each second-level items down into more detailed categories or tasks the team leader takes each second level item and asks what could go wrong with this? The various failure scenarios based on date past experience, or simple hunches or written on individual cards to form the third level of the tree. Next the fourth level of the diagram's used to describe various contingencies (countermeasures or preventive actions) that the team could utilize to minimize the impact of each failure scenario. In the fifth and final level of the chart the team evaluates these contingencies. The symbol X is typically used to mark those that are impractical while the symbol O is used to mark these that should be implemented (unmarked items are simply held for future consideration).

Failure mode and effects analysis (FMEA) is a slightly more sophisticated version of contingency planning

In FMEA steps, failure scenarios and contingency plans are typically described in more detail and the resulting information is displayed in tabular form. The key refinement is that each failure mode is then rated based on likelihood of occurrence and severity. These rating scores follow a Pareto distribution and direct the planning groups' attention toward the most likely and most severe potential failures.

Activity Network Diagram (the Arrow Diagram)

It shows the sequence of tasks required to accomplish some objective along with time estimates for each task. By compiling the time estimates a team can

- Define start and completion dates
- Identify the critical path of activities that dictate the
- minimum total time required to accomplish the objective.
- Manage the slack time in parallel tasks and monitor progress toward the objective written on this card.
- Based on the discussion the leader narrows from the factor of interest to every other item it influences. This process is repeated for each card in turn until all possible causal relationships have been documented.

The completed diagram gives us a greater appreciation of the system as a whole. Items with many outgoing arrows are key causal factors (Drivers) that if properly addressed influence a large number of other items. Identifying these drivers gives the team a sense of priorities or starting points in an otherwise overwhelming complex situation. Similarly, items with many incoming arrows are key effects. If the team properly addresses the many other driving (causal) factors on the diagram it should see changes in those key effects as a result. The team might want to track those few times as a way of assessing the ultimate success of the effort rather than trying to measure each of the causal factors directly.

The tree diagram (also known as systematic diagram) starts with an end result to be attained and then describes in measuring detail the full range of tasks or contributors to that result.

Graphically it resembles an organizational chart or family tree. To illustrate suppose that a planning committee in a home health agency has constructed a relations diagram and identified "availability of appropriate staff" as one of the key drivers in the causal system for patient satisfaction. This driver is written on a card and represents the first level of the tree the problem objective or goal statement. In the second level of the tree the group might break "availability of appropriate staff" into four categories of activity external recruiting internal transfers training programs and retention of existing staff. The comprehensive nature of these second level categories of team strives to be both complete and increasingly detailed as it moves down the levels of the tree. In the third level, the team takes each second level item and dissects it further into its component parts or necessary tasks, the dissecting process continues until the team reaches the point where tasks are defined well enough that they can be assigned to someone (typically this occurs at the third to fifth level of the diagram).

This group effort needed to construct the tree diagram ensures there are no major gaps in our thinking about what needs to be done and that in the end the people working on individual tasks will be able to see how what they are doing fits into a bigger picture.

Matrix Diagram – (Matrix, Matrix Chart)

The matrix diagram shows the relationship between two, three or four groups of information. It can also give information about relationship such as its strength the roles played by various individuals or measurements.

Six differently shaped matrices are possible

L.T.Y.X.C and roof shaped

Matrix data analysis /Priorities matrix

It is a complex mathematical technique for analysing matrices often replaced in this list by similar prioritization matrix. One of the most rigorous, careful and time consuming of the decision- making tools, a prioritization matrix is on L shaped matrix that uses pair wise comparisons of a list of options to a set of criteria in order to choose the best option(s).

Statistical and Design Tools Statistical Process Control (SPC)

A. This is a toolkit for managing processes. It is also a strategy for reducing the variability in products, deliveries, materials, equipment attitudes, and processes, which are the cause of most quality problems. S.P.C will reveal whether a process is in control, stable and exhibiting only random variation or out of control and needing attention. It also warns automatically, when performance deteriorates and can assist with long-term defect reduction. Identification of special assignable cause's reduction or elimination of causes of variation and achievement of a level of performance as close to target as possible.

B. Its categories variation according to the action needed to reduce it. To reduce common cause variation, one must act on the process.

To help distinguish between these two kinds of variation. Schewart devised the premier tool of SPC – the control chart. The simplicity of the control chart has inevitably led to its widespread and successful application in manufacturing and service industries.

Walter Schewart developed a theory of variation which forms the basis of SPC. The critical feature of Schewart's theory of variation is that

- Affinity Diagram (Affinity Chart, K. J. Method) – It organizes, a large number of ideas into their natural relationships. This method taps a team's creativity and intuition.

- Inter-relation or Relations diagram – The relations diagram shows cause and effect relationships. It helps a group analyses the natural links between different aspects of a complex situation.

- Tree Diagram (Systematic diagram tree analysis, analytical tree and hierarchy diagram) – It starts with one item that branches into two or more each of which branch into two or more and so on. It looks like a tree with trunk and multiple branches. It is used to break down broad categories into final levels of details. Developing the tree diagram helps one to move his thinking step by step from generation to specifics.

- Matrix Diagram

- Matrix data analysis/priority

- Arrow diagrams / Activity network diagram

Variation of this includes PERT (Program Evaluation and Review Techniques) chart.

Arrow diagram shows the required order of tasks in a project or process the best schedules for the entire project and potential scheduling and resource problems and their solutions. The arrow diagram lets one to calculate the critical parts of the project. This is the flow of critical steps where delays will affect the timing of the entire project and addition of resources can speed the project.

- Process Decision Program Chart (PDPC) – It identifies what might to wrong a plan under development. Counter measures are developed to prevent or offset these problems. By using PDPC, one can either revise the plan to avoid problems or be ready with the best response when a problem occurs.

Design of Experiments

A strategically planned and executed experiment may provide a great deal of information about the effect on a response variable due to one or more factors. Many experiments involve holding certain factors constant – and altering the levels of another variable. Key concepts in creating a designed experiment include blocking, randomization and replication.

A well performed experiment may provide answers to questions such as

- What are the key factors in a process?
- At what settings would the process deliver acceptable
- performance?
- What are the key main and interaction effects in the process?
- What settings would bring about less variation in the output?

Failure Mode and Effects Analysis (FEMA)

FEMA is a step by step approach for identifying all possible failures in a design, a manufacturing or assembly process or a product or service.

Failure modes, means the ways or modes in which something might fail. Failures are any errors or defects, especially ones that affect the customer, and can be potential or actual.

'Effects analysis' refers to studying the consequences of these failures.

Failures are prioritized according to how services their consequences are, how frequently, they occur and how easily they can be detected. The purpose of the FEMA is to take actions to eliminate or reduce failures, starting with the highest – priority ones. FEMA's are Process FEMA's and Design FEMA's

Creativity tools: This would include Brainstorming and mind maps.

Brainstorming (Nominal Group Techniques)

It is a group creativity technique by which efforts are made to a conclusions for a specific problem by gathering a list of ideas spontaneously contributed by its members. Some consider brainstorming is more effective than individuals working alone in generating ideas.

Brainstorming combines a relaxed informal approach to problem solving with lateral thinking. It encourages people to come up with thoughts and ideas.

The following steps are followed

- Prepare the group -:

The group should be small. Ideally it should be between 4-10.

Generally, people from wide range of disciplines, and include people, who have a variety of different thinking styles. A comfortable meeting environment for the session for this people.

- Present the problem -:

Clearly define the problem that is to be solved and lay out any

criteria that must be met. To make it clear that the meetings objective is to generate as many ideas as possible. All the participants must be given time to write down their own ideas. Then each one of them must be asked to share their ideas while giving everyone a fair opportunity to contribute.

- Guide the discussion -:

Later group discussion should take place for each idea. At the end of each idea voting is taken to eventually arrive at a consensus. During this process, there should be no criticism of ideas and creativity should be energized.

When managed well, brainstorming can help the organizations to generate radical solutions to problems. It can also encourage people to commit to solutions because they have provided input and played a role in developing them.

Mind Map

It is a diagram used to visually organize information. A mind map is often created around a single concept drawn as an image in the center of a blank landscape page to which associated representations of ideas such as images, words and part of words are added. Major ideas are connected directly to the central concept and other ideas branch out from those.

IV) Measurement Tools

Measurement is a core need for effective process management and therefore an important category for the quality profession. Tools such as Cost of quality, Benchmarking, Auditing, Surveys.

They enable one to collect and analyse different types of data that can then be used to guide and evaluate the effectiveness of improvement efforts.

Quality Circle (Q.C.)

- The concept originated in Japan
- Dr. Ishikawa presented the concept in 1962
- Quality circle is a small group of employees in the same work area or doing a similar type of work, who voluntarily meet regularly, periodically to identify, analyse and resolve work related problems, leading to improvement in their total performance and enrichment of their work life. (The issue should not be employee remuneration, working conditions, etc., for which separate channels should be used).

Employees doing the similar type of work are well familiar to problems faced by them. They are also in a position to offer suggestions to improve the same. It also enables the workers to participate in the improvement of their products, services and jobs, so building pride in their product and a sense of participation in and belonging to the organization. Quality circles recognize and use intellectual and practical potential of all the employees of an organization.

Objectives of Quality Circle

- Improvement in quality of product manufactured (service rendered) by the organization
- Improve mentation methods of production (service)
- Development of employees participating in Q.C
- Promoting morale of employees
- Respect humanity and create a happy work place worthwhile to work.

Main features of Quality Circle

- Voluntary Groups: QC is a voluntary group of employees generally coming from work area. There is no pressure from anywhere on employees to join QC.

- Small size: The size of QC is generally small consisting of six to eight members.

- Regular meeting: QC meetings are held once a week for about an hour on regular basis. The members meet during working hours, usually at the end of the working day in consultation with the manager. The time of meetings is usually fixed in advance in consultation with the managers and members.

- Independent Agenda: Each QC has its own agenda with its own terms of reference. Accordingly, each QC discusses its own problems and suggests corrective actions.

- Quality Focused: As per very nature and interest of QC, it focusses exclusively on quality issues. This is because the ultimate purpose of QC, is improvement in quality of product and working life.

Developing QC in an organization

- First requisite is the firm commitment from the top management in Quality Programme including QC

- Once decision is made a survey is conducted to find the feasibility and necessity of introducing QC.

- QC should be developed and introduced with great concern and precaution

- Publicizing the idea

Introduction of QC is just like an organizational change program. Hence like an organizational change program, the workers need to be convinced about the need for and significance of QC from the point of view of the workers and the organization. Moreover, participation in QC being voluntary its publicity among workers is necessary. To being with management should also arrange for initial training to those workers who want to form a quality circle.

Constitution of QC

Workers doing the same or similar type of work are drawn voluntarily to form quality circle. The members of QC is generally 6-8 members. The group selects a leader who co- ordinates the meetings. Once a QC is formed, they remain a permanent members of the circle unless they leave that work area.

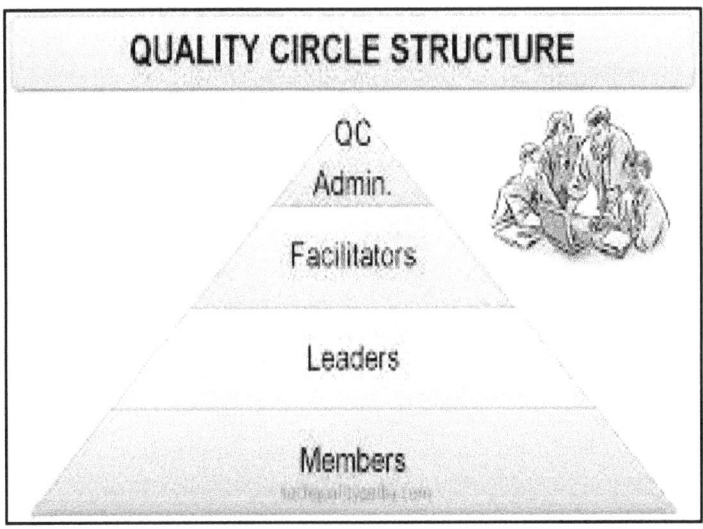

Problem analysis and suggested solutions

A list of problems using brain storming techniques.

Once the problem is identified the following steps are taken by the team.

- Define the problem
- Analyse the problem by collecting data
- Identify the cause
- Find out the root cause by data collection and analysis
- Identify the alternate solutions
- For see the probable resistance for implementation
- Decide on the best alternative

This is done on the basis of consensus of the team.

Presentation to and Approval of Suggestion by the Management

The final solution arrived at should be presented to the management is oral or written form. The management may evaluate the solution, by seeking clarification, or implementing the solution on a trial basis. Presentation of solution and later discussion helps improve the communication between the management and workers.

Implementation

Once the suggestion or solution is approved by the management, the same is put into practice in that workplace. The management may appoint a steering or co-ordination committee to successfully implement the solution.

Quality Circle in a Nutshell

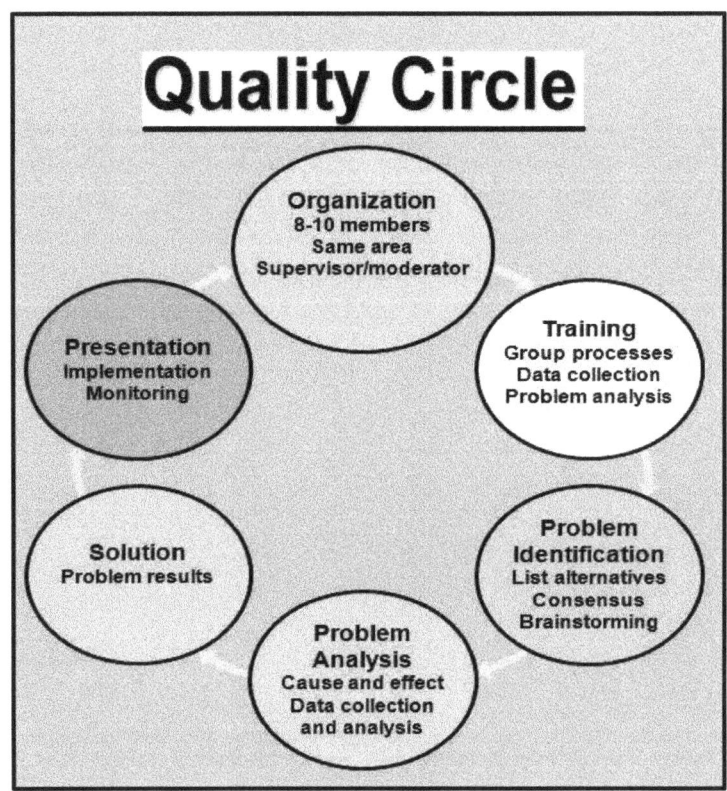

Q WHAT IS A QUALITY CIRCLE?
A group of 8-10 people who work on problems of their own choosing

WHAT'S IN IT FOR PARTICIPANTS?
- Learn New Things
- Job Satisfaction
- Fun
- Recognition

QUALITY CIRCLES

WHO CAN USE IT?
Interested in better quality of work life

HOW DOES A QUALITY CIRCLE WORK?

- Weekly Meetings
- Use of Problem Solving Method

Benefits of QC
Employees

- Improve their knowledge, communication, confidence and self esteem
- They learn to interact with and make presentation to the management
- Learn to work systematically after proper planning, and problems solving techniques
- Enrich the work life of employees, apart from attitudinal changes, cohesive team culture, etc.
- Improved working environment, happier relations with co-employees, greater job satisfaction are other benefits.

Organization

- Better implementation of the solutions because, being their solution, they take ownership.
- Improvement in Quality
- Cost effectiveness, better productivity and profits
- Improvement in organizational morale

Precautions to be taken while implementing QC. It is essential that management should implement the approved solutions sincerely, giving credit to the quality circle members. If for any reason suggested solutions cannot be implemented, the reasons for the same should be communicated to the members, appreciating the effort. If this is not followed, not only the

QC would fail in the organization, exactly the opposite impact will be seen in organization. The worker's confidence in management would be eroded and the morale would be negatively affected.

KAIZEN

Kai - Change - To break apart

To modify To change

Zen - Good -   Think about

Make good Make better

Kaizen means improvement, continues improvement involving everyone in the organizational form top management to managers, then to supervisors and to workers.

Kaizen is used by Japanese for any kind of improvement (both in private and working life). It is a philosophy. According to lmai, "Our way of life – be fit our working life, our social life or our home life – deserves to be constantly improved".

It is using common sense and is both a rigorous, scientific method, using statistical quality control and an adoptive framework of organizational value and belief, that keeps workers and management focused on zero defects. It is a philosophy of never being satisfied, with what was accomplished last week or last year. Improvements through Kaizen have a process focus. Kaizen generates process-oriented thinking is people oriented, is denoted at people's efforts. Rather than identifying employees as the problem, Kaizen emphasizes that the process is the target and employees can provide improvements by understanding how their jobs fit into the process and changing it.

A process emphasis goes beyond designing effective process, it requires the teams to understand why a process works, whether it can be modified or replicated somewhere else in the company and how it can be improved.

Comparison between Conventional approach and Process- emphasis approach

Employees are the problems	The process is the problem
Doing my job	Helping to get things done
Understanding my job	Knowing how my job fits in the process
Measuring individuals	Measuring performance
Change the person	Change the process
Correct errors	Reduce variation
Who made the error	What allowed the error to occur
Employees are the problems	The process is the problem
Doing my job	Helping to get things done
Understanding my job	Knowing how my job fits in the process
Measuring individuals	Measuring performance
Change the person	Change the process
Correct errors	Reduce variation
Who made the error	What allowed the error to occur

The message of Kaizen philosophy is that not one single day should go by in the organization, without some type of improvement being made in some process in the organization.

Kaizen deals with the management of change and is a methodology in the right direction to improve operations on a continual and incremental basis following the right steps.

- Establish a plan to change whatever needs to be improved.
- Carry out changes on a small scale
- Observe the results
- Evaluate the results and the process and determine what has been learned

The starting point for improvement is to recognize the need. The Kaizen principles emphasize problem – awareness and provide clues to identifying problems. When identified, problems must be solved. Thus, Kaizen is also a problem-solving process.

The three pillars of Kaizen are:

1. House Keeping: This is a process of managing workplace. For proper housekeeping, a valuable tool or methodology, the term FIVE S practices to a clean and manageable work area Sort Straighten Sweep Sanitize Sustain 5 S evaluations provide measurable insight into the orderliness of a work area and their checklist for manufacturing and non- manufacturing areas that cover an array of criteria as i.e. cleanliness, safety and ergonomics.

2. Waste (Muda) Elimination: The resources at each process – people and machines – either add value or not add value and therefore any non-value adding activity is Muda (waste). In Kaizen philosophy, the aim is to eliminate the seven types (7 deadly wastes), caused by Overproduction – Production more than production

Waiting – Poor balance of work – operation attention schedule Transportation – Long moves, re-stacking, pick up/put down Inventory unnecessary stock – Too much material

Over processing motion –

Defects – Material and labour are wasted Motion – Waiting to get parts because of space

Because eliminating Muda (waste) costs nothing. Muda elimination is one of the easiest ways for a company to improve its operations.

3. Standardization – Standards must be set by management but then should be able to change when the environment changes. Companies

can achieve dramatic improvement as reviewing the standards periodically, collecting and analysing data on defects and encouraging teams to conduct problem solving activities. Once the standards are in place and are being followed, then if there are deviations, the workers know, that there is a problem. Then employees will review the standards and either correct the deviation or advice management on changing and improving the standard. It is never ending process and is better explained and presented by the PDCA – or Deming cycle.

Kaizen practices and improves the statuesque by bringing added value to it. Kaizen does not or preclude innovation. Rather the two are complementary. It is top management's job to mountain the balance between Kaizen and innovation and it should never forget to look for innovation opportunities.

It practiced properly with full commitment from top management and participation of all employees. Kaizen practices can deliver breakthrough improvements in the range of 40-60%.

LEAN

Lean is a systemic method for the elimination of waste (Muda) within the manufacturing system (equally applicable to service delivery).

It also takes in account waste created through over burden (Muri) and waste created through unevenness in workloads (Mura).

Essentially lean is centred on making obvious what adds value by reducing everything else.

Lean manufacturing is a management philosophy derived mostly from the Toyota Production System (TPS) (Hence the term Toyotism is also prevalent). TPS is renowned for its focus on reduction of the original Toyota seven wastes to improve overall customer value, but there are varying perspectives on how this is best achieved.

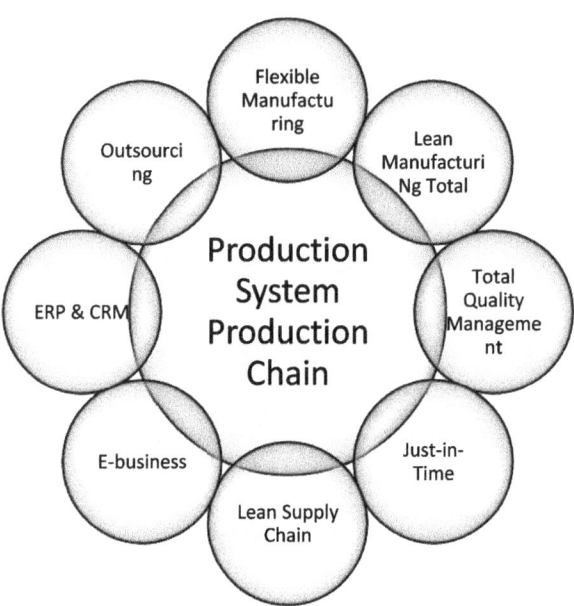

Lean Supply Chain
E-business

The core idea of Lean is to maximize Customer value, while minimizing waste. In other words, lean means creating more value for customers with fewer resources. A lean organization understands customer value and focusses the key processes to continuously impose it. The ultimate goal is to provide perfect value creation process that has zero waste.

Eliminating waste along entire value streams, instead of isolated points, creates processes that need less human effort, less space, less capital and loss time to make products and services, at for less costs and with much fewer defects, compared to traditional business systems. Companies are able to respond to changing customer expectations with high variety high quality, low cost with very fast through put times.

A popular misconception is that lean is suited only for manufacturing which is not true. Lean applies in every business and every process. It is not a tactic or a cost reduction production but a way of thinking and acting for an entire organization. Business in all industries and services, including healthcare and governments are using lean principles as they think and do.

To transform the entire organization the following issues to be addressed

- Purpose - What customer problems the enterprise, solve to achieve its own purpose of prospering?

- Process - How will the organization assess each major value stream to make sure, each step is valuable, capable, available, adequate, flexible and all steps are linked by flow, pull and levelling?

- People - How can the organization insure that every important process has someone responsible for continually evaluating that value stream, in terms of business purpose and lean process? How can one teaching the value stream be actively engaged in operating correctly and continually improving it? Lean thinkers need a vision before adopting lean tools.

Principles of implementation of Lean

- Specify value from the standpoint of the end customer by product family.

- Identify all the in the value stream for each product family, eliminating, whenever possible those steps, that do not create value.

- Make the value-creating steps occur in tight sequence, so the product will flow smoothly toward customer.

- As flow is introduced, let customers pull value from the next upstream activity.

- As value is specified, value streams are identified, wasted steps ae removed and flow and pull are introduced, begin the process again and continue it until a state of perfection is reached in which perfect value is created with no waste.

Seek Perfection

Map the Value System and Stream

Establish Flow

Create flow by eliminating flow

SIX SIGMA

Six Sigma is a set of techniques and tools for process improvement.

Six Sigma is a set of methodologies and tools used to improve business processes by reducing defects and errors, minimizing variation, and increasing quality and efficiency. The goal of Six Sigma is to achieve a level of quality that is nearly perfect, with only 3.4 defects per million opportunities.

It was introduced by Engineer Bill Smith while working in Motorola in 1986. Jack Welch made it central to his business strategy at General Electric in 1995. Today it is used in many industrial sectors.

Sigma seeks to improve quality of the output of a process by identifying and removing the causes of defects (errors) and minimizing variability in manufacturing and business processes. It uses a set of quality management methods and creates a special infrastructure of people within the organization.

Each six-sigma project carried out within an organization followed a defined sequence of steps and has specific value targets. For example, reduce, process cycle time, reduce pollution, reduce costs, and increase customer satisfaction and increase profits.

The Greek letter sigma is used to denote variation from a standard. The philosophy behind six sigma is that if you measure how many defects are in a process, you can figure out how to systematically eliminate then and get as close to perfection as possible. In order for a company to achieve Six Sigma, it cannot produce more than 3-4 defects per million opportunities (or 99.999% perfect) where an opportunity is defined as a chance for non-conformance.

There are two important Sigma process

- Six Sigma DMAIC – which

Defines the problem or project goal needs to be addressed

Measures – the problem and process from which it was produced Analysis – Data and process to determine root causes of defects and opportunities

Improves – the process by finding solutions to fix, diminish and prevent future problems.

Controls – Implement, control and sustain the improvements, solutions to keep the process on the new course. Controls the existing processes that fall below the six-sigma specification.

- Six Sigma DMADV which

Defines - the problem or project goal that needs to be addressed.

Measures - and determines customers' needs and specifications Analysis - the process to meet the customer needs

Designs - a process that will meet customers' needs

Verifies - The design performance and ability to meet customer needs New Processes or products that are trying to achieve Six Sigma quality

DMAIC	DMEDI
Used to improve existing processes, products and services.	Used to design new processes and products or to radically improve an existing process
Steps are: Define, Measure, Analyze, Improve and Control	Steps are: Define, Measure, Explore, Develop and Implement
Analytics and data driven	Data and statistical driven
Incremental improvement and reduction of variation	Breakthrough improvement
Shorter time frame than DMEDI	Longer time frame than DMAIC
Focuses on correction and improvement	Focuses on prevention
Focus on limited CTQs (Critical to Quality)	Broader focus on all those CTQs the customer deems important

- DFSS Process - It is a separate and emerging discipline related to Six Sigma quality process – It has five steps

Define - What the customers want or what they do not want

Design - a process that meets customers' needs

Optimize - Determine process capability and optimize the design Verify - Test, verify and validate the design

There are three key elements of Six Sigma Process Improvement

- Customers: They define quality. They expect performance reliability, competitive prices, on time delivery service, clear and correct transaction processing and more. This means it is important to provide what the customers need to gain customer delight.

- Process: Defining processes as well as defining their metrics and measures is the central aspect from the needs and processes, we can discover what they are seeing and feeling. This gives a chance to identify weak areas within a process and then we can improve them.

- Employees: The Company must involve all its employees to focus their talents and ability to satisfy customers. It is important that all team members should have a well-defined role with measurable objectives. They are assigned specific roles to play each with a title.

There are some roles to implement Six Sigma

- Sponsor: He acts as a problem solver. Sponsors are the owners of processes and systems who help initiate and co-ordinate Six Sigma improvement activities in their areas of responsibilities.

- Implementation Leader: He is responsible for supervising the Six Sigma effort.

- Coach: He is a Six Sigma Expert or consultant who sets a schedule defines result of project and who mediates conflict or deals with the resistance to program.

- Team Leader: He is responsible for overseeing the work of the team and for acting as a go between with the sponsor and the team members.

➢ Generates Sustained success
➢ Sets a performance goal for everyone
➢ Accelerates the rate of improvement
➢ Promotes learning and cross-pollination
➢ Executes strategic change

Benefits of Six Sigma

➢ 50% Cost reduction
➢ Cycle – time improvement
➢ Less waste of materials
➢ Better understanding of customer requirements
➢ Increased customer satisfaction
➢ More reliable products and services

Challenges

- Implementation of Six Sigma is expensive can take several years before a company begins to see the bottom line results.

All Six Sigma processes are executed by

- Six Sigma Green belts – Is given to a person less experienced than a Black belt person but is cost in a key role within a team.
- Six sigma Black Belts: The person possessing this belt has achieved the highest skill level, is an experienced in various techniques. He has completed a thorough internal program and has the experience of working on several project which are then overseen by Six Sigma.
- Master Black Belts: A person who deals with the team or its leadership but is not a direct members of the team itself.
- The Master Black Belt is available to answer procedural questions and resole the technical issues that come up.

Just In Time (Jit)

An inventory strategy, companies employ to increase efficiency and decrease waste by receiving goods only as they are needed in the production process, thereby reducing inventory costs.

This method requires that produces cost able to accurately demand.

The other terms JIT – manufacturing or JIT production is a methodology aimed primarily at reducing flow times within production as well as response times from suppliers and to customers. Alternate terms for JIT manufacturing have been – Short term cycle manufacturing (SCM), Continuous Flow Manufacturing (CFM) and Demand Flow Manufacturing (DFM).

JIT revolves around wastes. As its core JIT is a waste – elimination philosophy. The seven are Over Production Waiting Transportation, Processing itself, stocks (Inventories) Motion and Making Defective Products.

Some others maintain that JIT main aim is elimination of inventories. The following discussion is based on that concept. It gives hand in hand with concepts as Kanban, Continuous Improvement and Total Quality Management.

Highly advanced technological support systems need to be provided as the necessary back up that JIT manufacturing demands with production scheduling software and electronic data.

The following issues to be addressed while implementing JIT

- Management bay is and support at all levels of the organization are required.

- Adequate resources should be allocated, to obtain technologically advanced software.

- Building a close, trusting relationship with reputed and time-tested suppliers to minimize unexpected delays in the receipt of inventory.

- It requires commitment in terms of time and adjustments to corporate culture of JIT

- The design flow process needs to be redesigned and layouts needs to be re-formatted so as to incorporate just in time manufacturing

- Lot sizes need to be minimized

- Workstation capacity should be balanced whenever possible.

- Preventive maintenance should be earned out so as to minimize machine breakdowns

- Set up times should be reduced, wherever possible

- Quality enhancement programs should be adopted, so that

- total quality control practices can be adopted.

- Reduction in lead times and deliveries should be incorporated

- Motion waste should be minimized e.g. By incorporating conveyer belts

Advantages of JIT

- Keeps stock holding costs to a box minimum. The release of storage space results in better utilization of space and thereby bears a favourable impact on finances needed for such purpose.

- It eliminates waste out of date or expired products do not enter into the equation at all

- Only essential stocks are obtained, less working capital is required to finance procurement. Here a minimum re-order level is set and once that mark is reached, fresh stocks are ordered making this a boon to inventory management too.

- Due to low level of stocks held return on investment (ROI) would improve.

- As JIT production works on a demand-pull basis, all goods made would be sold, and thus it incorporates changes in demand with surprising case. This makes it appealing when market demands are volatile and unpredictable.

- JIT encourages the 'Right First Time' concept so that inspection and rework costs are minimized.

- High quality products and greater efficiency are delivered.
- Close relationships are fostered along the production chain.
- Constant communication with the customer results in high customer satisfaction
- Overproduction is eliminated.

Disadvantages of JIT

- JIT provides zero tolerance for mistakes which makes re-working very difficult in practice as inventory is kept to a base minimum.
- There is high reliance on suppliers, whose performance is generally outside the preview of manufacturer.
- Due to there being no buffers for delays, production downtime and the line idling can occur which would result in detrimental effect on finances and equilibrium of the production process.
- Transactions costs would be relatively high as frequent transactions would be made.
- Frequent delivers result in increased use of transportation.

JIT production requires intricate planning in terms of procurement policies and manufacturing process of if it is implementation is to be a success. Under JIT actual orders dictate what should be manufactured so that the exact quantity is produced at the exact time that is required.

KANBANKanban is a way for teams and organizations to visualize their work, identify and eliminate bottlenecks and achieve operational improvements in terms of through put and quality.

Kanban also spelt Kanban is a Japanese word for signboard or Billboard that indicates "available capacity to work".

Kanban is a concept related to lean and Just In time (JIT) production, where it is used as a scheduling system that tells one, what to produce, when to produce it, and how much to produce.

It is also a method to gradually improve whatever one does whether software development. IT, ops, Staffing Recruitment, Marketing and sales, Procurement – in fact almost any business function can benefit from Kanban to bring about significant benefits, such as reduced lead time increased throughput and much higher quality of products or services delivered.

In simplified terms, Kanban is a visual system for managing work, moving through a process – the "Value Stream', it is a system for visualizing work, reducing waste by limiting work in progress and maximizing customer value.

Three fundamental guiding principles of the Kanban are

- Start with what you have new – that is your current process
- Agree to peruse an evolutionary approach to change and improvement.
- Respect the current roles and responsibilities of the team/organization

Based on the above guiding principles, the following five practices are to be implemented

- Visualize the work and the workflow that follows
- Limit Work in Process (WIP) using a virtual Kanban System
- Manage flow
- Make Management Policies Explicit
- Use Models andthe scientific methods and improve collaboratively

To be effective Kanban, must follow strict rules of use e.g. Toyota has the following rules

- Later process picks up the number of items indicated by the Kanban at the earlier process
- No items are made or transported without a Kanban
- Defective products are not sent to the subsequent process. The
- result is 100% defect free goods.
- Reducing the number of Kanban increases the sensitivity.

Kanban cards a key component of Kanban and they signal the need to move materials within a production facility or to move materials from an outside supplier into the production facility. The Kanban card is in effect, a message that signals depletion of products or parts or inventory. When received, the Kanban triggers, replenishment of that product, part or inventory. Consumption therefore drives demand for production and the Kanban card signals demand for more product. So, Kanban cards help create a demand-driven system.

Three-Bin System

As example of a simple Kanban system implementation is a three-bin system for the supplied parts, where there is no in-house manufacturing. One bin is on the factory floor (the initial demand point) one bin is on the factory store (the inventory control point) and one bin is at the supplier. The bins, usually have a removable card containing the product details and other relevant information the classic Kanban card.

When the bin on the factory floor is empty (because the parts in it were used up in a manufacturing process) the empty bin and the Kanban card are returned to the factory store (the inventory control point). The factory store replant the empty bin on the factory floor with the full bin from the factory store, which also contains a Kanban card. The factory store sends the empty bin with its card to the supplier. The supplier full product bin with its Kanban Card is delivered to the factory store. The supplier keeps the empty bin. This is the final step in the process.

Thus, the process never runs out of product and could be described as a closed loop in that it provides the exact amount required with only one spare bin, so there is never over supply.

This "spare bin" allows for uncertainties in supply, use and transport in the inventory system. A good Kanban system calculates just enough Kanban cards for each product. Most function, that use Kanban, use the coloured board system (Heijunka Box).

Electronic Kanban

Many manufacturers have implemented Electronic Kanban (Sometimes referred as E-Kanban) Systems. These help to eliminate common problems such as manual entry errors and lost cards.

Jidoka

Jidoka highlights the cause of problems because work stops immediately when a problem first occurs. This leads to improvements in the processes that build in quality by eliminating the root causes of defects.

Automation describes a feature of machine design to effect the principle of Jidoka used in Toyota Production System (TPS). This type of automation implements some supervisory functions rather than production functions. This usually means that if an abnormal situation arises, the machines stop, and the worker will stop the production line. It is a quality control process that applies the following principles.

- Detect the abnormality
- Stop
- Fix or correct the immediate condition
- Investigate the root cause and install a counter measure

Automation aims to prevent the production of defective products, eliminate overproduction and focus attention on understanding the problems and ensuring that they do not reoccur.

POKA-YOKE

Poka – Yoke is a Japanese term that means "mistake proofing". It is any mechanism in a 'lean manufacturing' process, that helps an equipment operator avoid (Yo Kera) mistakes (poka).

Its purpose is to eliminate product defects by preventing, correcting or drawing attention to human errors as they occur. The concept was formalized, and the term adopted.

More broadly, the term can refer to any behaviour-shaping constraint, designed into a process to prevent incorrect operation by the user.

Poke-yoke can be implemented at any step of a manufacturing process, where, something can go wrong, or an error can be made.

VALUE STREAM MAPPING

In any job they may have three types of activities.

- Value Adding: The activity adds value to the intended objective
- Incidental Activities: They do not add value to the intended objective but essential for the business.
- Non-Value-added activities: They do not add any value nor essential for business. They are called waste (muda in Japanese)

In almost all value streams all the above three types of activities are knowingly or unknowingly are being performed. The objective should be to maximise the Value-added activities and eliminate or minimize the non-value-added activities.

For elimination of non-value-added activities one must know that how much and where such activities are performed. This can be discovered through value stream mapping. The main purpose of value stream mapping is to detect wastes.

Wastes are classified as

- Defects and Reworks
- Over Production
- Waiting – Idle time
- Transportation – Unnecessary
- Inventory – Excess
- Motion – Unnecessary movement
- Excess Processing

Value is expressed in terms of specific product (a good or a service or both at once) which means the customer's needs at a specific price at a specific time – as defined by the customer.

Waste is defined as "Any business activity that absorbs resources but does not add any value to the customer".

Value stream mapping is a diagnostic tool to assess the process. It is done by stakeholders and process owners, under the guidance lean experts to develop following documents.

- Current State Value Stream Map

Capturing the 'as is' operating practices, performed from the beginning to end. It identifies and measures the waste during the entire process. It helps in identification of opportunities for improvement.

- Value Stream Improvements Plan

Development of action plan and scheduling for making improvements to accomplish the future state value stream targets.

BENEFITS

- It helps to identify the deficiencies in the process and waste.
- Helps to identify the opportunities for improvement
- To develop action plan for improvements.

BENCHMARKING

- Benchmarking is the process of company one's business processes and performance metrics to industry bests or best practices from other companies.
- Benchmarking is the process of identifying and adopting outstanding practices from within the same organizations or from other business to help improve performance.
- It is also cryptically defined as 'A perfect of copying the business practices'.
- It is probably a very important exercise a company can do, when beginning the quality important process.
- Later it is also continues learning and improvement process, which ensures that the best practices are uncovered analysed, adapted and implemented, wherever appropriate.
- Dimensions typically measured are quality time and cost. Also, vital few, key successful factors and key performance indicators.
- In the process of best practices bench marking, management identifies the best time in their industry or another industry where similar processes exist and compares the results and practices of these studies (the targets) to one's own results and processes.
- Successful companies may be from Malcom Baldridge Award Winners, Deming's prize winning or accredited institutions.

- Benchmarking is used to measure performance using a specific indicator (e.g. Cost per unit of measure, productivity per unit of measure, cycle time of x per unit of measure, or defects per unit of measure) resulting in a metric of performance that is then compared to others.

Procedure: There is no single benchmarking process that has been universally adopted. One such suggestion

12 Stage methodology consists of

- Select Subject
- Define the process
- Identify potential partners
- Identify data success
- Collect data and select partners
- Determine the gap
- Establish process differences
- Target future performance
- Communicate
- Adjust goal
- Implement
- Review and recalibrate
1. Review
2. Identify and Understand your process
3. Agree what and who to Bench mark
4. Plan and Action Improvement s
5. Analyse Data & Identify gaps
6. Collect the Data

Following is another example of benchmarking methodology

- Identify problem areas: Since benchmarking can be applied to any business process or function a range of research techniques may be required. They include informal conversation with customers, employees or suppliers, exploratory research techniques such as focus groups or in-depth marketing research quantitative research, surveys, question, process mapping quality variance reports, financial ratio analysis, performance indicates etc. Before embarking on comparison with other organization it is essential to the functioning and processes of the organization.

- Identify other industries that have similar processes – Hospitals having processes to transfer patients from surgery to recovery rooms.

- Identify organizations that are leaders in these areas – Look for the very best in the industry. Consult customer's suppliers, financial analyst's trade association and magazines. To take above example, minimum time and smooth transfer without any problems or discomfort to the patient.

- Survey companies for measures and practices. Companies target specific business processes using detailed surveys of measures and practices used to identify business process alternatives and leading companies. Surveys are typically masked to protect confidential data by neutral associations and consultants

- Visit the best practices, compares to identify leading edge practices. Companies typically agree to mutually exchange information beneficial to all parties in a bench marking group and share the results within the group.

- Implement new and improved business practices. Take the leading-edge priorities and develop implementation plans which include identification of specific opportunities funding the project and selling the ideas to the organization for the purpose of giving demonstrated value from the process.

Bench Marking Protocol

- It should be legal, should be willing to give and share the information with others. Keep information internal, and not to share it with others, without the permission of the organization from when it is taken. To be honest and it should be followed with full commitment from all the conceived personnel.

Types

- **A.** Internal – Comparing performance between different groups or teams within an organization
- **B.** External – Comparing performance with companies in a specific
- **C.** industry and across industry.
- **D.** Process Benchmarking
- **E.** Financial Benchmarking
- **F.** Performance Benchmarking
- **G.** Product Benchmarking
- **H.** Functional Benchmarking
- **I.** Best in Class Benchmarking
- **J.** Operational Benchmarking
- **K.** Energy Benchmarking

Use of Benchmarking

- Mission and Vision Statements and customer(client) Surveys (77% of the organization) of 20 improvement tools
- SWOT Analysis – 72%
- Informal Benchmarking (68%)
- Performance Benchmarking by 49%
- Best Practice Benchmarking by 39%

Benefits

- It sets performance goals
- It helps to accelerate and manage change
- It improves processes and performance
- It allows the employees to see the "Outside the Box'
- It generates an understanding and following the best practices including world class performance.

Business Process Re-Engineering

(BUSINESS PROCESS REDESIGN, BUSINESS MANAGEMENT, BUSINESS CHANGE MANAGEMENT)

Business Process Re-engineering (BPR) involves the radical redesign of care business processes to achieve dramatic improvements in productivity, cycle times and quality.

In Business Process Re-engineering companies start with blank sheet of paper and rethink existing processes to deliver more value to the customer. They typically adopt a new value system that places increased emphasis on customer needs.

BPR aims to help organizations, fundamentally rethink how to do their work in order to dramatically improve customer services cut operational costs and become world close competitors.

Companies reduce organizational layers and eliminate unproductive activities in two key areas. First they redesign functional organizations into cross-functional teams. Second they use technology to improve data dissemination and decision making.

BPR is a dramatic change initiative that contains five major steps Managers shield

- Refocus company values on customer needs
- Redesign care processes, often using information technology to enable improvements.
- Reorganize a business into cross functional teams with end to end responsibility for a process.
- Rethink basic organizational and people issues.
- Improve business process across the organization

As we can see BPR is different from other approaches to organization development, especially TQM or CQI movement, by virtue of its aim to fundamental and radical change rather than iterative improvement.

BPR derives its existence from different disciplines and four major areas can be identified as being subjected to change in BPR – organization, technology, strategy and people – where process view as used as common framework for considering three dimensions.

Companies use Business Process Re-engineering to improve performance, sustainability on key processes that impact customers. BPR can

- Reduce costs and Cycle Time: by eliminating unproductive activities and the employees, who perform them. Reorganization by teams decreases the need for management layers, accelerates information flows and eliminates the errors and rework caused by multiple handoffs.

- Improve quality: By reducing the fragmentation of work and establishing clear ownership of processes. Workers gain responsibility for their output and can measure their performance based on prompt feedback.

BPR has its own critics – who termed it – basically downsizing the workforce. Recent developments prefer Business Management Process to BPR.

BUSINESS PROCESS MANAGEMENT (BPM)

BPM is a field of operations management that focuses on improving corporate performance by managing and optimizing a company's business processes. It can be described as a Process Optimization Process.

BPM enables organizations to be more efficient, more effective and more capable of change than a functionally focused, traditional hierarchal management approach. These processes can impact the cost and revenue generation of an organization.

The goal of BPM is to reduce human error and miscommunication and focus stakeholders on their requirements of their roles

Association of Business Management Professionals defines BPM as BPM is a disciplined approach to identify, design execute, document, measure, monitor and control both automated and non-automated business processes to achieve consistent, targeted results aligned with an organization's strategic goals.

BPM involves the deliberate, collaborative and increasingly technology aided definition improvement, innovation and management of end to end business processes that drive business results, create values and enable an organization to meet its business objectives with more agility.

BPM enables an enterprise to align its business processes to its business strategy leading to effective overall company performance through improvements of specific work, activities either within a specific department, across the enterprise or between organizations.

Business Process Management activities can be arbitrarily grouped into:

- Design: Process design encompasses both identification of existing processes and the design to be identification process. The proposed improvement could be human to human, human to system workflows and might target regulatory, market or competitive challenges faced by the business.

- Modelling: It takes the theoretical design and introduces combination of variables (e.g. Material costs). It may involve 'what if analysis'.

- Execution : To combine software and human intervention to get most optimum process.

- Monitoring: It encompasses the tracking of individual processes, so that information on their state can be easily seen and statistics on the performance of one or more processes can be provided.

- Optimization: It includes retrieving performance, information from modelling or monitoring phase, identifying the potential or actual bottlenecks and the potential opportunities for cost saving or other improvements and then applying those enhancements in the design of the process.

- Re-engineering: BPR may be used to achieve efficiency.

- Suites: A market has developed enterprise software leveraging the business process management concepts to organize and automate the processes.

Quality Function Deployment (QFD)

QFD is a structured approach to defining customer needs or requirements and translating them into a specific plans to produce products to meet these needs. The 'voice of the customer' is the term to describe these stated and unstated customer needs or requirements.

QFD is a method developed in Japan to help transform the voice of the customer (VOC) into engineering characteristics for a product.

According to the original developer QFD is a method to transform qualitative user demands into quantitative parameters to deploy the functions forming quality and to deploy methods for achieving the design quality into subsystems and component parts and ultimately to specific elements of the manufacturing process.

QFD is applied in a wide variety of services, consumer products. QFD consists of two components which are deployed into

designed process.

- Quality Deployment Component brings the consumer's voice into the design process.

- Function Deployment component links different organizational functions and units into the design to manufacturing transition via the formation of design teams

- Process of QFD – Four phases

- Product concept planning: It starts with customers and market research with leads to product plans, ideas sketches, concept models and marketing plans.

- Product Development and specification: It would lead to development of proto types and tests.

- Manufacturing process and products tools: They are designed based on the product and component specifications.

- Production of Product: It starts after the pilot has been resolved.

After the products have been marketed, the customer's voice is taken again.

BENEFITS OF QFD

- Attends to the voice of customer.
- Good co-ordination between product planning and production process.
- Product will be more competitive
- Continuous improvement in the product because customer's voice will be based as an ongoing process.

Value Engineering (VE)

Value Engineering (VE) is a systematic method to improve the value of goods or products and services by using an examination of function.

Value is defined as the ratio of function to cost.

Value can therefore be increased by either improving the function or reducing the cost. It is a primary tenet of value engineering that basic functions be preserved, not to be reduced as a consequence of perusing value improvements.

VE is a function oriented systematic team approach and team approach and study to provide value in a product, system or service. Often this improvement is focussed on cost production on cost reduction. However other important areas such as customer perceived quality and performance are also of paramount importance in value equation.

Value Engineering techniques can be applied to any product process procedure system or service any kind of business or economic activity including health care, governance, construction industry and in the service sector.

The reasoning behind value engineering is as follows: If marketers expect a product to become practically or stylishly obsolete within specific length of time, they can design it to only last for that specific life time. The products could be built with higher grade components, but with VE, they are not because this would impose an unnecessary cost on the manufacturer and to a limited extent also an increased cost to the purchaser. VE will reduce these costs. A company will typically use the least expensive components that satisfy the products' requirements. Due to short life span, which is often a result of VE, planned obsolescence has become associated with product deterioration and inferior quality. That is why many have criticised this model because of its economic and societal implications.

VE is applied by a structured decision-making process to assess the value of procedures and services. The procedure involves following eight phases:

Orientation,

Information,

Function,

Creativity,

Evaluation,

Recommendation,

Implementation and

Audit.

Benefits of VE

- Lowering of operating and Manufacturing costs
- Improving quality management
- Simplifying procedures
- Minimizing paperwork
- Lowering staff costs
- Increasing procedural efficiency
- Optimizing construction expenditure
- Developing value attitudes in staff
- Competing more successfully in market place.

Education And Training

"If I am asked to cut a tree in eight hours, I spend six hours in sharpening the knife".

This is true in many spheres but more so in quality management. Japanese excellence in quality was due to their focus on training.

The term training refers to a learning process that involves the acquisition of knowledge, skills and competencies as a result of the teaching of vocational or practical skills and knowledge that relate to specific useful competencies.

The importance of training in the successful implementation of quality management programs is widely acknowledged as an essential component.

The training must be for everybody starting with the top team and cascading down the organization through training and education, a common language is achieved throughout the organization. Responsibility of organizing the training program must be entrusted one person for better co-ordination and uniformity. Training should be held regularly and must be compulsory. It is the responsibility of the management to schedule the program in such a way that the normal work is not affected.

For quality program to be effective it must be planned in a systematic and objective manner. It must be continuous to meet not only about technology, but also about environment and the changes that are taking place. It must be not only about the standard processes but also about organizational goals and policies and behavioural aspect.

Quality Policy must be decided first and communicated to everyone Quality training objectives must be set, taking into account the specific quality training needs of the individuals and groups. Then the methodology, duration and content must be planned. The training should be internal and external trainers – who themselves are well trained. Training must be focused, so that people receive appropriate courses at the appropriate level of their needs. It must also include quality skills and techniques. The employees undergoing training must be provided with training materials. In one steady it was found that 4-6% of total working hours or 90-120 hours or 12-15 days every years is most optimum that each employees should receive training.

Training should include, concept of quality, problem solving techniques, statistical process control methods to reduce waste and process control methods to reduce waste, and process simplification and steady of customer expectation and feedbacks.

Feedback from the employees receiving training must be taken. Evaluation of the program and the benefits to the organization. Should be carried out periodically. Necessary modifications may be made in the program.

Leadership in Quality

Effective leadership is essential to establish and sustain effective quality management in the organization.

Leadership is the process of influencing group activities, towards accomplishment of goals in a given situation. Leadership is responsible for promoting commitment in an institution, which is the foundation for effective quality program.

Leaders have multiple roles to achieve this goal like – to be a source of inspiration, motivate, to develop team work, creating harmonious relationship to be a model and to lead the team.

He acts as a mentor, facilitator innovation coordinator, monitor, coach, teacher and director.

A leader must be skilled at articulating a vision for quality improvement. The leaders must create a common of priorities. They must create an aligned understanding of priorities, among all stake holders. They must also be able to good relations among all employees, by creating mutual trust. Leaders should also set proper process to achieve the quality goals.

The role of leadership within quality comprised of the following factors

- Be proactive and lead through example rather than dictating. True leaders lead in a way that in a way that is active in implementing and following through an actions, rather than simply dictating actions without leading by examples.

- Understand and react fluctuations in the external environment.

The external is every bit as important as internal environment which is why leaders need to fully comprehend and correctly react to various changes within this environment

- Consider the wants of all stake holders: from customers to owners, employees, suppliers, local communities and general public – these stake holders form a vital part of the quality management process and can greatly affect the organizations' success if there is no relationship and understanding from leadership point of view.

- Establish a clear view of the organization's prospects. A clear view of the organizations' future is essential in order to accurately plan ahead by continuously changing goals and milestones in the future

- Establish common values and ethical role models throughout the organization – Leaders instil a sense of values and day ethics that are entrenched in the organizations' mission statement acting as role models, to be a part of quality management initiatives based on these common values.

- Develop trust and Eradicate fear – a good company relies on effective leadership to develop trust across internal and external environments, without the need to use fear as a motivating factor. Equip employees with the needed and freedom to strive for duly and accountability

- With a well-developed range of strategies that all levels within the organization, along with resources that equip employees to meet the organization's goals, the entire organization can be involved in improving quality across the board.

- Inspire, motivate and recognize contributions from all levels of employees – the ability and motivate staff across all levels allow employees to be actively involved and invested in quality management initiates.

- Foster open and honest communication: Communication is essential in order for all levels within the organization to work together to implement improvement strategies and as leader, the role is to foster open communication from all employees.

- Teach, train and coach employees : through learning and coaching on various improvement strategies and other initiatives, employees are able to gain a better understanding not only on what they are doing, but why they are performing their tasks.

- Develop challenging objectives and targets through goal setting, leaders are able to foster constant growth and development across the organization by continually improving the standards of goals within each department.

- Implement clear initiatives and strategy to bring these goals into function once goals have been set, leaders implement these goals accordingly to involve all levels in quality campaigns across organization.

To summarize the leadership role

- Set personal example of practicing what you preach about quality
- Establish a quality vision and translate it into mission statements
- Institutionalize the initiative and not individualize
- Instil in every employee a sense of pride in the work he/she does.
- Empower employees
- Document every process to create a manual for conformance
- Devise systems that on function even if the individuals change
- Use external quality audits to benchmark efficiency of the systems
- Customers' complaints to be monitored, analysed and attended to immediately
- To measure customer satisfaction levels to generate ideas
- Delegate specified decision making powers down the line
- Improve communication at all levels
- Provide transparency in information
- Focus on preventive rather than curative maintenance
- Develop quality culture in the organization

Cost Of Quality

It is a team that is widely used – and widely misunderstood. It is a common perception that higher the quality of the product, more expensive it is. Sometimes it is also presumed that a costly product is always better. But the cost of quality has a different dimension. The reason quality has gained prominence is that organizations have gained an understanding of the high cost of poor quality. Quality affects all aspects of the organization and has dramatic cost implications. The most obvious consequences, occurs, when poor quality creates dissatisfied customers and eventually leads to loss of business.

Quality has several costs. They can be divided into two categories.

A. Quality Control Costs: They consist of costs necessary for achieving high quality. They consist of

- Prevention costs : They are costs incurred in the process of poor quality from occurring they include
  - ➤ Quality Planning Costs, such as the costs of developing and implementing a quality plan.
  - ➤ Costs of product and process design from collecting customer information to designing processes that achieve conformance to specifications.
  - ➤ Employee training in quality measurement is included under this heading.
  - ➤ Costs of maintaining records of information and data related to quality
  - ➤ It is found in some studies, one hour of planning and education saves, 10 hours of problems and confusion
  - ➤ Prevention and doing it right the first time are the key to provide quality at a most economical way.

- Appraisal Costs: are incurred in the process of uncovering defects.

They include –
- Cost of quality inspections
- Product testing
- Performing audits to make sure that quality standards are being met.
- Costs of worker time spent measuring quality and the cost of equipment used for quality appraisal.

B. Costs of Failure of Control (Costs of non-conformance): There are some who describe, the cost of quality is not the price of creating a quality product or service. It is the cost of NOT creating a quality product or service.

Non-conformance costs are costs from products or services are not conforming to requirements or customer/user need. They are divided into

- Internal Failure Costs – They are associated with discovering poor product quality before the product reaches the customer site.

One type of internal failure is

- Rework/Scrap – It is the cost of correcting the defective item.
- Sometimes the item is so defective it cannot be corrected and must be thrown away. This called scrap and its costs include all the material labour and machine cost spent in providing the defective product.
- Other types are cost of machine downtime, due to failure in the process and costs of discounting defective items for salvage value.

- External Failure Costs:

They are associated with quality problems that occur at the customer site. These costs can be particularly damaging because customer faith and loyalty can be difficult to regain. They include

- Customer Complaints
- Product repairs and returns
- Warranty claims
- Recalls
- Litigation costs, resulting from product liability issues.
- Lost sales and lost customers

External failures can sometimes put a company out of business almost overnight. Organizations that consider quality important, invest heavily in prevention and appraisal costs in order to prevent internal and external failure costs. Earlier defects are found, the less costly they are to correct. External failure costs tend to be particularly high for service organizations. The reason is that with a service the customer spends much time in the service. The customer spends much time in the service delivery system and there are fewer opportunities to correct defects than there are in manufacturing. It is interesting that, according to Deming, 85% of the problems are created by people, who never teach the product.

The cost of Quality is easy to measure in production areas and difficult in service areas. The cost can exceed 25% of the sales revenue which may appear surprising. But this is because 90% of the non-conformance costs are invisible.

Cost of implementing quality programmes is far less than the costs of not implementing it. Cost of implementing, quality management is less expensive by greater productivity and lower total product and service cost. Hewlett Packard company discovered that rework and dealing with customer complaints cost the company 20% revenues and involved time and effort of 25% company employees. Cost of not doing things right for the first time for a typical service organization is equal to around 40% of the total operating costs. For the whole decade of the 1980's about 1/3 of all the work performed by all American Companies was actually rework because of quality problems. These examples show the importance of cost of quality and measures to be taken to keep it as low as possible.

Cost of quality is zero – Is a stunning statement. What is means is the cost of quality is not the price of creating a quality product or service. It is the cost of NOT creating a quality product or service. In other words, if product or service is produced or delivered without any defect or deficiency – no extra cost is necessary for quality. That is why it is said, 'cost of quality is zero'.

Quality Audit

It is a process of systemic examination of a quality system, carried by audit team. Audits are an essential management tool to be used for verifying objective evidence processes to assess how successfully process have been implemented for judging the effectiveness of achieving any defined target levels, to produce evidence concerning reduction and elimination of problem areas.

Audits are

Statutory: Compulsory to carry out audits.

Voluntary: It is the choice of the organization. Some accrediting agencies expect that audits should be carried out e.g. ISO.

Audits – can be

Internal – from personnel within the organization External – From External Agencies

Quality are typically performed at predetermined time intervals and ensure that the institution has clearly defined internal system monitoring procedures linked to effective action. This can help to determine if the organization completes with the defined quality system processes and involves procedural or result based assessment criteria.

Audits are carried out by organizations in different areas of their centres. E.g.

- Inventory audit
- Employees or the way they perform
- Management audit
- Data Quality audit

Audits – give report about

- Non-conformance
- Corrective Actions

- Good Practices
- Suggestions for improving process and controlling mechanisms Quality Audits – help the organization
- To know the status of conformance
- To take corrective actions
- To make necessary changes – for continual improvement
- To advertise to the public and to improve the sales

Quality Audits can be an integral part of compliance or regulatory requirements – e.g. US FDA requires quality auditing to be performed as part of its Quality System Regulation (QSR) for medical devices.

Some countries (New Zealand, Australia, Sweden, Finland, Norway, UK and USA) have adopted quality audits in their education system. It focuses on procedural issues, rather than on the results or efficiency of a quality system implementation.

Audits are used for safety purposes. It is an effective way to avoid complacency and it focuses not only on compliance but also on effectiveness.

In the recent times, the process and tasks, that a quality audit involves is managed using a wide variety of software and self-assessment tools.

Legal Compliance and Quality Management

One of the requirements the products or services must meet provide quality is

- Comply with applicable regulations and standards

The Accrediting agencies require legal compliance for granting the same.

Thus, it is essential that manufacturing of a product or delivery of a service to strictly follow, and adhere to all the applicable laws, regulations, rules and acts. The authorities expect everybody to comply them to ensure safety and welfare of the society. There may be regulations in some fields to ensure quality in the product or service. These laws and regulations differ from industry to industry. But broadly they relate to

- Environment
- Safety of the workers
- Overall policies of the state
- Consumer interest and safety
- Quality of the product and service

In order to cut the cost, there may be practice of resorting to shortcuts. But real quality management should ensure, compliance of all legal provisions.

Legal compliance for hospitals is detailed in the second part.

Licensing, Certification, Accreditation and Awards

After implementing quality management system, many organizations opt for third party evaluation and recognition, to reassure itself and to project to their customers both existing and potential.

Licensing is also a third party certification for following all the regulations laid down by the authorities. They are compulsory and obtaining these licenses is a precondition to carry out the activities. Nowadays large number of licenses are required both in manufacturing and service sectors.

The Certification, Accreditation and Awards are voluntary. The organization may choose to get them or apply to be selected.

Certification: Third party certification is an independent assessment of an organization, offers assurance that the organizations has met the requirements pertaining to a product, person or management system.

Third party certification means that an independent organization has reviewed the manufacturing process of a product and has independently determined that the final product complies with specific standards for safety, quality or performance.

This review typically includes comprehensive formulation/ material reviews, testing and facility inspections.

(The above definition is also applicable to service in place of product)

Most certified products bear the certifiers mark on their packaging to help consumers and other buyers make educated purchasing decisions.

There are many certifying bodies for different areas. But these bodies should have some credibility. They must be accredited bodies themselves.

e.g., Integrated Quality Certification Pvt. Ltd.

QMS Certification Agencies

Accreditation

Accreditation is the process in which certification of competency, authority or credibility is presented.

Organizations that issue credentials or certify parties against official standards are themselves are formally accredited by accreditation bodies. Hence, sometimes they are known as Accredited Certification Bodies. The accreditation process ensures that their certification practices are acceptable, typically meaning that they are competent to test and certify third parties behave ethically and employ suitable quality assurance.

Accredited entities must provide evidence to the accreditation body that they conform to the standards. Accreditation is used for understanding the Quality status of an organization. Accreditation status indicates the standards of quality as set by the Accreditation agency are met in relation processes and outcomes (wherever applicable).

There are several Accrediting Bodies like

JCAHO - Joint Commission on Accreditation Healthcare Organizations

NABH - National Accreditation Board for Hospitals and

Healthcare Awards and Prizes

They are given periodically (usually every year) for excellence in that field. Whereas certification and accreditation can be obtained by several organizations who meet the criteria, prizes and awards are very few in number.

Eg Malcolm Baldrige Award Deming Prize

Some of these related to health field will be discussed in detail in a later chapter.

Quality In Service Sector

Quality management was more focussed on manufacturing sector. Later it was realised that it is equally important, perhaps more so, that quality plays a vital role in service industries. It is estimated a large percentage (60%) of employees work in service sector.

Compared to product quality, it is usually very difficult to define measure and control service quality. Traditionally serve quality has been defined as the difference between customer expectations of services to be received and perceptions of the service actually received. Hence the service quality is the most part related to the process delivering services. The increasing bargaining power of customers in services is necessitating the inevitability of providing quality service. The service quality can only be measured by customers and spread through word of mouth. It is very dangerous, and it immediately damages the profit of the company if something goes wrong. Hence, constant improvements and controls are strongly needed in order to produce a high quality service without any deficiencies. The best way to clarify and recognise the attractive factors of services to the customers is to listen to them and learn from them. The management needs constantly adopt new strategies to meet their expectations. The service quality helps the companies to lower costs through decreasing deficiencies and the high quality services help the companies to gain competitiveness through excellent reputation, attraction and loyalty of customers.

Dimension of Services Quality

Dimension	Definition	Example
Tangibles	Appearance of physical facilities, equipment, staff and communication materials.	Does the service have pleasant offices?
Reliable	Ability to perform the promised service-	Is the contracted

Dependability and accuracy service always delivered?

Responsive- ness

Willingness to help clients and prompt service

Do service staff always try and help you?

Competence Possession of the required skills to perform the service

Are the staff good at their job?

Courtesy Politeness, respect, consideration and friendliness of staff

Do staff treat you with respect?

Credibility Trust-worthiness, believability and honesty of staff

Do you trust the staff?

Security Freedom from danger, risk or doubt

Do you feel safe using the service?

Access Approachability and ease of contact

Is the service easy to get to?

Communication Keeping clients informed in language they can understand and listening to them

Do staff inform you about your treatment?

Knowing the Client Making efforts to know the clients and their needs.

Do you think staff know your personal needs?

Special features of Service Quality Managing Service Delivery

Service quality is affected, not just by the fitness of the product, but also by the manner of delivery.

Perishability

Planning services requires careful matching of the capacity to demand and this can be difficult to achieve. Unlike manufactured goods, services cannot be stored.

Interaction between producer and consumer

Customers seldom participate in manufacturing organizations, whereas in service organizations interaction between the organization and the consumer is high. Interaction affects perception of quality. Perceptions of quality in service organizations often lead to 'moments of truth' - when the producer and the consumer meet. Such moments are critical because they can be engineered to promote satisfaction or, if mismanaged, can have the opposite effect.

Service organizations are expected to deliver a constant standard day in and day out. Many services must be performed 'on demand' even though conditions may be far from ideal. They are also relatively labour-intensive and therefore vulnerable to the effects of interactions between employees, who are frequently required to work without immediate supervision. Service organizations must further contend with customer moods and behaviour and interaction among the customers.

Intangible nature of quality

Service quality is a subjective issue. A customer's perception of quality may rest upon factors which have little to do with either the product or the manner of its delivery. This means there are critical elements of service quality over which the organization can at times exert little or no control.

Important service industries are hotel, transport, education, Health care, etc.

Quality In Health Care

Like, quality in general what is quality in health care is also not easy. Again, the individual understands it but does not know how to explain the same. It means different things to different people. Some patients think that quality health care means, seeing the doctor right away, being treated courteously by the doctor or hospital staff or hearing the doctor spend a lot of time with the patient and family.

While the hospital understands and agrees that these things are very important, but it believes that clinical quality of care is even more significant. The reason is offering high quality evidence- based care leads to more lives 'saved and less time in the hospital.

Quality health care is also doing the right thing (getting the health care services the patient needs), at the right time (when one needs it) in the right way (using the appropriate test procedure and treatment) to achieve the best possible results.

The Institute of Medicine defines health quality by following attributes

- Safety: patients should not be harmed by the care that is intended to help them
- Patient Centred – Case should be based on individual needs
- Timely: Waits and delays in case should be reduced
- Effective: Care should be evidence based
- Equitable: Care should be equal to all patients.

It defines 'health care quality as the degree to which health services for individuals and populations increase the likelihood of desired health outcomes and are consistent with current knowledge.

This definition suggests that

- Quality performance occurs on a continuous theoretically ranging from unacceptable to excellent.
- The focus is on services provided by the health care delivery system

Quality In Healthcare

- Quality may be evaluated from the perspective of individuals or populations
- Research evidence must be used to identify the services that improve health outcomes.
- In the absence of scientific evidence regarding effectiveness, professional consensus can be used to develop criteria.

Characteristics of Quality Health Care	
Safe	Avoiding injuries to patients from the care that is intended to help them
Effective	Providing services based on scientific knowledge to all who could benefit and refraining from providing services to those not likely to benefit (avoiding underuse and overuse, respectively)
Patient-Centered	Providing care that is respectful of and responsive to individual patient preferences, needs, and values and ensuring that patient values guide all clinical decisions
Timely	Reducing waits and sometimes harmful delays for both those who receive and those who give care
Efficient	Avoiding waste, including waste of equipment, supplies, ideas, and energy
Equitable	Providing care that does not vary in quality because of personal characteristics such as gender, ethnicity, geographic location, and socioeconomic status.

'Quality in health care is the total package of features and characteristics of a health care service or product, and the way in which it is provided, that bear on its ability to satisfy the agreed needs of the purchaser within the constraints imposed by professional judgments, at the lowest cost, whilst minimizing waste and losses'.

Quality is multidimensional. It has many contributing factors. It is not easily summarized in a simple, quantitative way. Some aspects of quality can be measured objectively, such as time spent for waiting to see a doctor, some may not, such as the doctor's manner during consultation. The most easily measured criteria are not necessarily the most important.

Quality is subject to constraints. Assessment of quality in most cases cannot be separated from costs. However, cost may be wider than the simple financial cost: it refers to any critical resources such as people, tools and tike. Some resources will be more constrained than others, and where there is a high demand for a resource that is heavily constrained, the availability of that resource will become critical to overall quality.

Quality is about acceptable compromises. Where quality is constrained, and compromises are required, some quality criteria may be sacrificed more acceptable than others: e.g. comfort may be sacrificed for productivity.

Quality criteria are not independent. The quality criteria interact with each other causing conflicts. For example, the greater the number of patients assigned to a clinic, the longer the waiting time during the clinic, but shorter the waiting time to get an appointment. In this case, a conflict exists between the two desirable attributes.

Acceptable quality changes over time. Progress in clinical practice and improvements in care mean that levels of performance deemed to be satisfactory are constantly being raised. This is an increase in both actual capability and in public expectation.

While approaching an understanding towards quality one should try to recognize the distinct difference between the quality of design and quality of the delivery. A particular service may have a very high design quality, but be delivered badly, or conversely, may have poor design quality but is delivered superbly.

The uniform, high standards for patient care and safety are designed to be adaptable to local needs, thus accommodating legal, religious and cultural factors within a country. Standards address the following areas:

- Access to Care and Continuity of Care
- Patient and Family Rights
- Assessment of patients
- Care of Patients
- Patient and Family Education
- Quality Management and Improvement
- Prevention and Control of Infections

- Governance, Leadership, and Direction
- Facility Management and Safety
- Staff Qualifications and Education
- Management of Information.

In the health field, Maxwell (1984) identified six dimensions of quality health care as:

- Access - patients have reasonable access to services in terms of geographical convenience, waiting time for treatment, physical design of buildings, and availability of transport.
- Relevance of need – the services provided are appropriate to the needs of the local population.
- Effectiveness – the services actually achieved the intended benefits and outcomes.
- Equity - services are even-handed between different patients and social groups.
- Social acceptability - the services are proved in ways (including customer relations, style of services, flexibility, and impact on the community at large) which are acceptable to the population served.
- Efficiency and economy - the service is provided in such a way as to give value for money (QALY).
- -Zifko-Baliga, et al., expand upon Maxwell's model, linking 15 perceived quality dimensions to it in the Donabedian form in the following manner:

Structure Building/Technological Environment Amenities – Parking

Billing Procedures

Process Professional Expertise

Physician Validation of Patient Beliefs Interactive Communication Image

Process Interactive Caring

Nurses Professional Efficiency Individual Reliability

Process Interactive Caring

Nurse   Professional efficiency Individual Reliability

Process Insight, Acumen

Support Staff Skills

Outcome Physical

Emotional Cure

Donabedian identified three components of health care as:

- Technical care- the application of the science and technology of medicine to the management of personal health care problem.
- Interpersonal relationship – the social and psychological interaction between client and practitioner.
- Amenities – décor, temperature, equipment, food etc.

Donabedian's model implies that quality healthcare requires a blend of sound technical training and skills provided for service users within a culture, which understands and responds to consumers' needs. This holistic approach to the definition of quality ties in well with the "better management, better health" model.

Donabedian also suggested the structure, process and outcome model for measuring the level of quality.

- Structure – the characteristics of the care setting.
- Process - what is done for the patient.
- Outcomes – how the patient responds to care.

Structure includes:

- Safety code compliance
- Equipment maintenance
- Physical access
- Personnel certification, training and continuing education
- Disciplinary oversight for staff

- Hours of operation
- Scheduling
- Telecommunications and information systems. Process includes:
- Technical, clinical quality of care
- The quality of the interpersonal interaction between patient and provider
- Access to care
- Appropriateness of care

Process measurement captures several dimensions: clinical (or technical) quality, interpersonal quality, access to care, and appropriateness of care.

Technical quality refers to the provider's clinical knowledge and skill, and the proficiency of the processes of care that the patient received.

Interpersonal quality refers to the interaction between the provider and patient. It encompasses communication, the responsiveness of the provider to the patient's concerns, and the "caring" aspect of providing care. While some people still regard interpersonal quality as a "luxury" item or superficial concern, studies have shown that patients who have better communication with their doctors achieve a better therapeutic response.

Access to care and the appropriateness of care capture the utilization issues that are a key part of the process of care dimension. The fee for service system raised concerns that providers had clear financial incentives to give more services than were appropriate or necessary. Concerns about the excessive use of services proved to be well founded, and in addition to leading to an increase in costs, the overuse of services conveyed a measurable risk to patients. The excessive, inappropriate use of unnecessary services represents an **error of commission**.

Under managed care, in countries like the U.S.A., however, concerns are being raised about potential **errors of omission,** where indicated services are not provided. To facilitate access to care, the barriers that inhibit patients from receiving services must be identified. While most barriers are financial, there are other well-documented factors that block or impede access to indicated services, such as geographic distance, racial and ethnic characteristics, patient education, language, and immigration status.

Determining who is accountable for errors of omission will become increasingly complicated in a heavily managed care environment – especially when there is scientific uncertainty about the clinical value of the services.

Outcomes:

They indicate how a patient is doing as a result of care. On the negative side, this dimension is commonly thought of as having

five facets.

- Death
- Disease
- Disability
- Discomfort
- Dissatisfaction

The measurement of outcomes is intended to determine how the patient fared as a result of treatment. For example:

- Did the patient live? For how long?
- Has the patient's health improved?
- Can the patient function normally?
- Is the patient in pain? Is the pain controlled?
- Is the patient satisfied with the care received?

The ideal definition of quality would need to have the merit of removing the idea of quality being a luxury, at the same the understanding it from the health industry point of view where it is not easily quantifiable, accessible and tangible. However, some of the mystery of quality in healthcare could be removed if we think of quality as representing conformity to some standard against which we can measure it is advance. For example, even if a manager is hindered by lack of resources he may still be able to meet certain standards.

Picker Methodology: Understanding Patients' Experience

Understanding the patient's experience of illness and health care requires, first of all understanding how patients perceive their needs. What is lit about their interaction with providers, systems, and institutions that patients say matters to them and affects them, either positively or negatively? Through focus groups, focused interviews, and national surveys the Picker Institute has spent much of the last decade exploring the experiences of patients who have been treated in a variety of clinical settings, including hospitals, clinics, and doctors' offices, and who represent a broad range of ages, ethnicities, geographic locations, and medical conditions. Based on this work, the Institute has identified eight "dimensions" of care to be especially critical, from the point of view of patients:

- Access: Patients want access to care and they are frustrated by the barriers they often encounter - whether because of telephone triage or voice mail systems; scheduling difficulties; zealous "gatekeeper"; or restrictions imposed by managed care or insurance coverage.

- Respect: patients describe a sense of anonymity and loss of identity in hospital and clinic settings and a strong need to be recognized and treated with dignity and respect as individuals. They also worry about how their sickness or treatment might affect their lives, and they want to be both informed about and involved in the medical decisions.

- Coordination: Patients have a unique vantage point on the processes of care. Their perceptions of the competence and efficiency of their caregivers are shaped, in large part, by how well clinical care, ancillary and support services, and "front-line" care are coordinated.

- Information, Communication and Education: Patients often express the fear that information is being withheld from them, that they are not being completely or honestly informed about their illness or prognosis. In particular, they emphasize the need for information about their clinical status, prognosis; information about the processes of care; and information that helps them manage on their own away from the clinical setting.

- Physical Comfort: One of the most immediately disturbing aspects of illness is the physical discomfort and disability it brings. Physical care that comforts patients, especially when they are acutely ill, is one of the most elemental services that care givers can provide, from the patients' perspective. Patients also report a heightened awareness of cold, frightening, or gloomy institutional trappings and a parallel appreciation of clean, comfortable, and pleasant surroundings.

- Emotional Support: The fears and anxieties that illness provokes can be as debilitating as the physical effects. In particular, patients express anxiety about their illness and fears about possible outcomes or long-term prognoses; worries about the impact of their illness on their ability to care for themselves or their dependents; and concerns about the costs of medical care or the impacts of illness on their family income.

- Involvement of Family, Friends: Patients rely on family members and close friends for social and emotional support, to serve as advocates or proxy decision-makers, and often as the primary caregivers when they are away from clinical settings. They also worry about the repercussions of their illness on friends and family.

- Transition and Continuity: Patients often experience a discontinuity of care as they move back and forth between inpatient, outpatient, and home care settings. They do not understand the institutional and functional boundaries and find it difficult to negotiate the system effectively.

Measuring Healthcare Quality - Challenges

To some degree quality is in the eye of the beholder

It also means balancing the competency views and needs of different stakeholders like patients, physicians and purchases (providers).

- Patients: They tend to evaluate care in terms of its responsiveness to their individual needs they expect that medicine is able and willing to solve most health problems, medications can cure any number of physical and psychological problems, surgery can undo the damage caused by genetic factors, lifestyle choices or accidents and immunizations can prevent the development of diseases that until recently meant death or disability.

Patients' expectations about the health care system may differ from that of other stakeholders which may lead to different evaluations of quality. Providers' emphasis on cost control may be negatively viewed by patients. Shorter visit lengths, which reduce the cost may have a negative effect on patient's ability to participate in making choices about their care. On the other hand, many aspects of technical quality of care cannot be evaluated by patients and they are not rated highly by them on humanness, responsiveness or satisfaction.

- Physicians: They are caught between efforts to control costs, their own judgment about the best course of treatment for a patient and demands that patient's values be reflected in making treatment choices.

These three influences do not always lead to the same conclusions. Cost control frequently is achieved as third parties make decisions about what services will be covered and what types of providers can offer those services. Involvement of third parties in decisions making may diminish the importance of physician judgment and autonomy which may lead physicians to conclude that the technical quality of care is suffering.

- Providers': From the providers' perspective, quality represents a way of evaluating how well the resources (mainly financial) are being utilized. The cost consciousness implies greater concern about unnecessary use of services. It also includes their concern about patient's satisfaction malpractice and perception of poor quality, costly treatment, which all affect the utilization and occupancy of the hospitals sooner or later.

The challenge for quality assessment is to find a way to balance the above competency expectation and demands on the health care system. A starting point is to make explicit what all stakeholders value and regards as an essential mission of health care. Areas of agreement among these perspectives ought to define the control focus for quality measurement. Areas in which objective is not shared by all groups but is not necessary in conflict with other expectations should be incorporated into the quality measurement system next. Areas of direct conflict require solutions outside the quality assessment arena.

PROBLEMS ASSOCIATED WITH THE MEASURING OF HEALTH CARE SERVICES:

- Variability of objectives: Improvement of efficiency v/s improvement of objectives.
- No tangible products: No direct reliable source of evaluation, but through customer satisfaction and complaints.
- Levels of education and variety of objectives: different type of personnel with varying qualifications, skills land experience.

PROBLEMS IN PROCESSING DATA FOR ASSESSING QUALITY:

- Lack of comparability of data.
- No consensus on correct indicators.
- Lack of historical data: to compare institutions over time.
- No link to provider action: measures are often 'poor' measures of provider quality as they are not linked to provider action e.g. the emotional state of a patient a year after surgery may not depend on quality of the surgeon or hospital where the surgery was performed.
- Difficulty in collection of data as there is no integrated system.
- Vulnerability to manipulation: Performance on indicators may be a 'gamble' e.g., a surgeon being measured by on 'unadjusted'

mortality for bypass surgery; could 'artificially' inflate the measure by performing surgery only on low risk patients.

Importance is given to outcome data in any study based on quality. However, it has got its own drawbacks, as outcome data is not without its limitations and complexities.

- Indicators are not equally relevant to all procedures. A critical indicator for one may be irrelevant for the other. E.g. mortality is a primary outcome for bypass patients because a meaningful change of death exists, but it is irrelevant for tonsillectomy patients as such patients rarely die.

- Though statistically relevant, some indicators frequency may not be sufficient to generate statistically significant comparison. E.g. blood loss in TURP patients occur infrequently.

- Relevance of indicators varies due to the deferring treatment goals of the patient; one patient may wish to maximize length of life the other may wish to maximize the quality of life e.g. one patient chooses radical mastectomy to eliminate fear of reoccurrence, another may choose lumpectomy to minimize the disfigurement.

- Some indicators may have an inverse relationship. Optimizing one indicator may negatively affect another indicator e.g. Minimizing mortality may actually increase the morbidity as those patients who would have otherwise died suffer from major complications.

- Risk factors to be adjusted for mortality are different for different complications e.g. the mortality of surgery patients varies with the morbidity and severity and type of complication.

- Outcomes often do not point towards specific process of care that requires modification e.g. mortality rate does not tell the provider which aspect of care needs to be improved. (quality is all about improving processes)

- Outcomes tracked after a long period of time may be as a result of natural progress of disease e.g., chronic cardiac patient may ultimately have a MI as a natural course of the disease and not as a result of poor medical care.

- Positive outcomes of treatment often correlate with patients' compliance of physicians' recommendations e.g. bypass patients' recovery depends upon willingness to quit smoking, changing of life style, minimizing of stress etc. patients who refuse to do this may require a repeat procedure.

- Family history, environmental conditions are important variables in assessing potential outcomes of treating a disease.

- Difference in how indicators are defined render comparison across institutions difficult e.g. Infection rates may vary across institutions due to non-standard definition of infection.

- Critical data is often difficult to track without linked data system facility. Inconsistent patient identification numbers, improper linkages hamper the flow of information e.g. an unanticipated return to the emergency department is a valuable indicator but can only be tracked if the visit is captured on a central data source.

- Some indicators are impossible to track without community data base e.g. repeat procedures, readmission rates are valuable indicators but are easily undercounted if the patient goes to another physician or hospital.

- Some incidences of stroke may be so short lived that they may be missed e.g. some incidences of stroke may be so short lived that they may be missed.

- Different patients respond to the same data request in a different manner e.g. patients tolerate pain differently land will report different pain scores.

- Indicator may inadvertently create incentives to artificially inflate the measure e.g. physicians may be encouraged to treat less severe patients.

- An indicator is only as good as the measuring instrument. If the measuring instrument is incorrect or poorly executed, the indicator is meaningless. E.g. the number of PAP smears performed is meaningless if the quality of the laboratory is poor.

- Focusing on the quality of a few procedures can create incentives to ignore other indicators e.g. in measuring caesarean section rates, physicians and the hospital staff may pay attention on caesarean section rates ignoring the quality of vaginal deliveries.

- The choice of specific outcome measures can vary widely across stakeholders representing different perspectives. For example, for some employers, the most important outcome is whether (and when) the patient returns to work. For the patient, the most important outcome may be quality of life.

- Preference for certain outcomes is also specific to each patient. For one patient with widespread cancer, for instance, the preferred outcome may involve being kept comfortable, even if that means an earlier death. For another patient with the same extent of cancer, the preferred outcome may be prolonging life at all costs, even if that means further discomfort caused by the side effects of treatments.

- Some outcomes are easier to measure than others. For example, while it is relatively simple to measure the number of deaths, it is difficult to measure (let alone define) quality of life.

- Another problem with measuring outcomes is that the results of hospital care that are of greatest importance, such as when the patient returned to normal functioning or to work, often do not occur until days, weeks, or months after the patient has left the hospital. It is not always clear whether these outcomes can be attributed to the care received at the hospital.

- While the improvement of patient outcomes is the ultimate goal of providing health services, there are drawbacks to looking exclusively at outcomes. For example, there is little that doctors can do currently to alter the course of a stroke unless the patient arrives at the hospital immediately after the stroke has occurred – and even if the patient arrives immediately, the exact treatment is still controversial. Should hospitals be held accountable for something beyond the reach of current medical therapeutics? Further, not all outcomes can be linked definitively to therapeutic interventions. If such a link cannot be established, it is not clear whether the outcome can be improved.

- The process of delivering health care in an inpatient setting is extraordinarily complicated, involving not only a long string of interpersonal interaction but also the application of highly technical knowledge. The same interaction may be judged very differently depending on whose perspective is used. For example, even doctors who are marginally competent and behind-the-times on their medical knowledge can be loved by their patients because they take the time to interact with them on a personal level. Thus, if these doctors were to be judged on the technical process of care, serious deficiencies might be found, but when the same doctors are evaluated based on general patient satisfaction, their patients would be completely content with the doctors' performance. Conversely, patients can experience bad outcomes with their care, and be dissatisfied, even when everything was done perfectly from a technical viewpoint.

- Another issue is that different units within the same hospital may have varying levels of quality performance. For example, a hospital that offers excellent obstetrical care may not be as capable at performing orthopaedic surgery. For that reason, many researchers argue that it is unrealistic and inappropriate to assign a single, summary score to represent a hospital's overall quality.

Evolution Of Quality in Health Care

- BC 2100 BE Hammurabi

When penalty for surgical malpractice was to amputate the hands of the surgeon. This code focused basically on bad care. Unlike recent times when establishment and maintenance of minimum standards.

- Florence Nightingale addressed the link between poor hospital sanitation and the high – 47% fatality rate among wounded soldiers during the Crimean war 1854. She introduced hand washing, sanitizing surgical tools, regularly changing bed linens and making sure all wards were clean. She also promoted good nutrition and fresh air. By those measures mortality had come down to 22%.

- Dr. Ignaz Semmelweiss – A Hungarian physician was known as Saviour of Mothers. He discovered that the incidence of puerperal fever could be drastically cut by the use of hand disinfection in obstetrical clinics. Mortality of this illness between 10% to 35%. Dr. Semmelweiss proposed the practice of washing hands with chlorinated lime solutions. His records showed that by adopting that practice the incidence of mortality was reduced to less than 1%.

Some of the Nightingale's specific improvements were, the reduction of overcrowding (beds had to be spaced three feet apart) provision of ventilation, the removal Calvary horses that were being stabled in the hospital basement assuming the sewers leading from the hospital were flushed several times a day and disinfecting latrines/drains with beat charcoal. She documented meticulously. Her method of recording was to the present day statistical quality measurement and she was an innovator in the collection, tabulation, interpretation and graphical display of descriptive statistics.

Seven years later, Sanitary Commission was founded. Clara Barton and Dr. Elizabeth Blackwell, patrolled Union Army camps, inspecting the living conditions and the hospitals organized diet kitchens. These Sanitation Agents were considered to be critical to the success of Union Army during the Civil War.

Louis Pasteur - who discovered that disease was caused by micro-organisms. It led to wide-spread adoption of antiseptic practices by physicians and hospitals.

Another innovator was Surgeon General Dr. Blue, who was responsible to combat Influenza and plague outbreaks. His tools were quarantine (including ships entering the country) mandatory medical examinations of all immigrants entering the country.

Communication in the form of weekly newsletters that continued information about the outbreaks and the results of influenza research conducted at the laboratory.

Dr. Blue is viewed to be a kind of visionary quality leader, needed in the event of global disease pandemics of the future. The medical records continue to be the most researched archival documents.

Dr. Ernest Codman, was a pioneering Boston surgeon. He is the acknowledged founder of outcomes management in patient care. He followed the progress of patients through their recoveries in a systemic manner. He kept track of his patients via "End Result Cards" which contained basic demographic data, along with the diagnosis, the treatment and outcome. Each patient was followed up for at least one year to observe long term outcomes. He also believed that this information should be made public so that patients could be guided in their choices of physicians and hospitals.

He also helped in founding the American College of Surgeons and its Hospital Standardization Programme. The latter eventually became Joint Commission on Accreditation of Health Care Organizations.

The modern quality movement has since transformed to include a wide variety stakeholders, a range of unique and modified approaches and an evolving set of goals.

Many efforts were made to outline the deficiencies in the delivery of healthcare. It prompted numerous and multidimensional efforts towards health care improvement. They included re- engineering and restructuring of systems of health care delivery, encouragement of peer review. They included identification and improvement of medical processes, constant improvement, and evaluation of performance and public reporting of quality data.

The modern physician is the product of a long textbook and apprentice process. Quality is based almost solely on the skills of craftspeople. And craft traditions are virtually blind to system to systems issues central to modern management concepts related to quality in healthcare.

It is not patient variation, but inconsistent quality of care that generates the widely quality of care that generates the widely variable patient outcomes from region to region.

American college of surgeons (ACS) founded in 1913 started addressing he great variations in quality. By 1917, ACS developed and started the Hospital Standardization Programme (HSP). HSP was a set of uniform, high standards to physicians practicing at hospitals seeking the distinction of achieving the standards. The unit of quality assessment was poor case review. Following a death or other adverse outcome physicians gathered to review the record and discuss the case. They assessed, whether the outcome might have been preventable. This learning based model of quality assurance successfully improved hospital standards.

Flexnor Report - 1910

- Avedes Donabedian conceived structure – process outcome there According to him quality is a product of two factors –

One is the science and technology of providing care and Second is the application of first factor in practice.

He proposed that components of quality in health care consisted of efficacy, effectiveness, optimality, legitimacy, equity and acceptability.

1950-1960 – JCO adopted Donabedian's and created quality assessment and improvement framework based on physical and staffing characteristics of caring for patients, the method of delivery and the results of care over the years, JCO's mission grew to embrace most healthcare settings.

USA – Government Regulatory Programme.

- State Licensing programs provided in 1800s
- 1906 – FDA undertook the national regulation of medication
- 1935 – Medicare was institutionalized mandatory principles central to hospital operations, staff credentialing, round the clock nursing care and utilization review.
- 1980's – Healthcare Quality Improvement Initiative allowed professional standards review organizations to apply patient care algorithm to claims history and data to set to serene cases and describe how well the conforms to establish guidelines.

All RQ have emerged providing excellent models for quality care. Evidence based practice was started by Archie Cochrane in 1950's. It became apparent that it was not effective to train and encourage clinicians to independently find and apply best clinical practices.

Quantitative systematic reviews began to appeal to the physician's scientific outlook over qualitative suggestions. This eventually paired the way for health care to embrace the six sigma and lean frameworks.

Since 1980's there has been steady transition from a needs based to an efficient profit making industry by adopting quality concepts like TQM, quality trilogy and zero defects. Influence of Quality Gurus on other industries also spread to healthcare and the health care industry started applying the principles of TQM, CQI and other concepts.

Since 1980's there have been many efforts, to improve the quality in health care. Apart from good clinical care, the focus is on safety and patient's rights. Various quality processes and means were adopted by the industry, like TQM, CQI, Six Sigma, Lean was also gradually practiced in health care sector also. All over the world the focus is on health care quality.

In India too, the scene has been changing in last four to five decades. Initially it was thought that quality management was needed and was applicable to other industries but not to healthcare industry. Gradually it was realized that they are relevant to health care institutions. Since 80's many hospitals obtained ISO' certification. In next decade hospitals received JCI accreditation. Quality Council of India was established under its supervision. NABH accreditation was initiated. There are several hospitals have been accredited by NABH. Similarly, laboratories can be accredited under NABL. The hospitals and other health care institutions have realized the importance of the quality in health care. It has become 'Mantra' of both in Government and Private Sectors.

Importance Of Measuring Quality of Care

To help consumers and purchasers make informed choices about health care:

Information on quality can help consumers make informed choices. Most consumers know little about the technical proficiency of the physicians and other health care providers they choose. Some ask friends for referrals. Some choose providers based on limited information available with their family physician. Some choose providers based on convenience of location. When selecting health plan, consumers may compare price and covered services, but they can find it difficult to learn how well plans provide care in general or for particular conditions. Quality monitoring can provide such information to help consumers decide where and from whom to obtain it.

Information on quality can also help public and private group purchasers of care. Companies that provide health insurance for their employees must decide which health plans to make available. Similarly, with the dawn of health insurance on the horizon it can be decided which health professionals can provide care to beneficiaries of health insurance. As concerns have increased about rising health care costs, many large purchasers have considered price of care as the primary factor in determining which health plans to offer. Yet, while it is tempting to believe that more efficient plans trim; costs in health care while keeping essential and necessary services. Research has not shown this to be true. Instead, studies reveal cost containment to be a blunt instrument that, by itself, results in the elimination of both necessary and unnecessary care. Quality assessment and monitoring provide the tools we need to balance cost and quality.

To help physicians and patients make informed treatment and referral decisions:

Information on quality is also useful for physicians and patients when making specific treatment and referral decisions. However. In many hospitals, the success rates are not as good as in the studies, which often include only the best clinicians and facilities and enrol patients who have no other diseases and who are likely to follow treatment instructions carefully. Because care provided in the "real world" may not have the same results as care provided under research conditions, information on local surgeons' individual results will help primary care providers and patients determine which available surgeons at which hospitals have the best success rates and, given those rates, whether the potential benefits outweigh the risks. If the surgical success rates at available hospitals are low enough, a non-surgical alternative, such as treatment with medications alone, may turn out to be a better option.

To help clinicians and health plans improve their care.

Clinicians and health plans can use information concerning their own quality of care to improve the car they provide. Monitoring quality provides the opportunity not only to address inferior quality, but also to identify and learn from examples of superior quality. Health plans may find that they need to help individual clinicians improve their care, or they may identify organizational problems that hinder provision of high quality care. Clinicians and plans may welcome the opportunity to improve, and those that might not otherwise address quality problems may be motivated by public reporting to address them.

To determine the impact of new policies and systems:

The health system is rapidly changing because of private market forces and public policies. However, we know relatively little about the impact of these changes on the health of the population. Sometimes we cannot even predict whether and change will increase or decrease quality because the change creates multiple, competing incentives for the various participants in the system.

To provide clinical input to financial decision making process:

Cost-cutting efforts create incentives for health plans to reduce the amount of care provided, which may actually improve the health of the population when useless or harmful care is eliminated. However, when necessary, care is cut, health may decline. Quality of care criteria can help guide decisions about which type of care should be maintained and which type might be safely eliminated. Better decisions should result in the delivery of a more effective package of services.

Importance And Benefits of Quality In Hospitals

IMPORTANCE
- Health as an indicator of quality of life and the life and death situations of patients in hospitals.
- Just in time style of functioning where the patient is the input, process and also the output. Thus, a deficiency at any given time would adversely affect the outcome.
- Increased awareness among the masses.
- Role of legislation and Insurance with the entry of concept of HMOs.

BENEFITS
- Increased customer satisfaction.
- Empowered employees.
- Higher revenue for the organization. (The Deming Chain Reaction)
- Lower costs as a result of getting it right the first time and reducing undesired situations.

Other important potential benefits include the ability to:
- Concretely demonstrate to employees and the community at large the hospital's strong commitment to honest and responsible provider and corporate conduct;
- Provide a more accurate view of employee and contractor behaviour relating to fraud and abuse
- Identify and prevent criminal and unethical conduct;
- Tailor a compliance program to a hospital's specific needs;

- Create a centralized source for distributing information on
- health care statutes, regulations another program directives
- related to fraud and abuse and related issues;
- Develop a methodology that encourages employees to report potential problems;
- Develop procedures that allow the prompt, thorough investigation of alleged misconduct corporate officers, managers, employees, independent contractors, physicians, other health care professionals and consultants;
- Initiate immediate and appropriate corrective action; and
- Through early detection and reporting, minimize the loss to the Government from false Clair and thereby reduce the hospital's exposure to civil damages and penalties, criminal sanction and administrative remedies, such as program exclusion.

Finally, in health care, production and consumption are inseparable. The services are consumed when they are produced, which makes quality control difficult. This necessitates that marketing and operations functions occur simultaneously. In short, the management of health care quality cannot be separated from the management of its provision. The customers usually serve as participants in the service act.

How to set up Quality Management Systems

Whatever be the type of the health care institution, primary, secondary or tertiary diagnostic or standalone organization, basic principles are same.

The institutions should have a clear, precise, unambiguous goals and objectives. The same should specify the quality policy and objectives. These should be communicated to every stakeholder. Most of the problems and failures are because of improper, insufficient information to the employees.

To install the quality management system the planning should start ideally even before the institution is set up. If the organization is already functioning, some modifications would be necessary.

Implementing Quality Program involves the following three steps.

- Quality Planning
- Establish Quality goals
- Identify who the customers are
- Determine the needs of the customers
- Develop product features that respond to customers' needs
- Develop processes, able to produce the product features
- Establish process controls, transfer the plans to the operating forces
- Quality Control
- Evaluate actual performance
- Compare actual performance with quality goals
- Act on the difference
- Quality Improvement

- Prove the need
- Establish the infrastructure
- Identify the improvement projects
- Establish project teams
- Provide the teams with resources, training and motivation to
➤ Diagnose the causes
➤ Stimulate remedies
- Establish controls to hold the gains

Broadly the following are the sequential steps need to be taken.

- Commitment from Top Management Full understanding, support and involvement of management. It means not just the commitment of requisite resources, but a leadership role by the management.
- Educating the Management and staff
- Formation of Quality Management Team
- Awareness campaign and Development of Quality Culture
- Defining Key, Improvement Objectives
- Development of Quality Policy and Quality Manual
- Training of Top Management
- Training of Lower Level Staff
- Identification and Mapping of all the organization process
- Development of Hospital Information System
- Formulation of criteria and standards
- Implementing the program
- Management Review of the QMS
- Internal Audit and Mock Survey

- Detection of Non-confirmative measures
- Review and Implementation of corrective measures
- External Certification / Accreditation

Following the above broad steps and principles setting up quality management system involves three main areas –

Process

Structure Described below Outcome

After setting up structure and process, it is important to define the measurable elements beforehand in both clinical and non-clinical areas. The management and staff should be made aware of them before hand, so that they function to get the best possible outcomes.

Structure

There are standards about the physical structure of various facilities. The areas, height of ceiling, interiors, electrification connection, colours, humidity, air cycles, etc. It is also better to look into adjuncies other than making changes later, unless it is inevitable.

Once the physical structure is ready, it is necessary to plan and install all the medical equipment's and other machinery. While obtaining and installing them it is essential to follow all the regulatory and safety norms. There are standards, about their numbers specifications.

When the physical infrastructure is getting ready, parallelly, it is very important to do manpower planning. Appointment of optimum number of staff with right credentials is very essential. They must be provided with necessary training. There must be planning to organize training for them periodically in technology, soft skills and quality assurance.

According to Donabedian Structure includes all the factors that affect the context in which care is delivered. This includes the physical facility, equipment and human resources as well as organizational characteristics such as staff training and payment methods. These factors control how providers and patients in healthcare act and are measures of the average quality of care, within a facility or system structure is easy to observe and measure and it may be the upstream cause of problems identified in the process.

Processes

Much more important than the above infrastructure is setting up proper processes and systems, both for clinical and non-clinical areas. First it is necessary to list all the tasks and functions. Then the standard operative procedures to be prepared taking inputs from the actual users and other stake holders. The SOPs should not only detail the normal processes to be followed in those circumstances.

The SOP manuals should be prepared and made available to all the users. Every staff number should be given training ensuring that he has necessary understanding skill and motivation to follow the SOP's. Periodic review and retraining is also essentials. All the time of setting up structure and Process, it is mandatory to follow all the statutory and regulatory provisions. Apart from this, ethical considerations like confidentiality, patients safely and rights must be followed at all levels.

Apart from SOP's measuring the quality performance and outcomes should also be defined in advance and communicated to the concerned people. The criteria should be objective and subjective element should be minimal. Perhaps the only exception, but most vital is the feedback from patients.

According to Donabedian process is the sum of all actions that make up healthcare. These commonly include diagnosis treatment, preventive care and patient education but may be expanded to include actions taken by patients and their families. Process can be further classified as technical, processes, how health care is delivered, or interpersonal process in which all encompasses the manner in which care is delivered.

According to Donabedian, the measurement of process is nearly equivalent to measurement of quality of care, because process contains all acts of health care delivery.

Information about process can be obtained from medical records, interviews, patients and practitioners or direct observations of healthcare visits.

A good management system is required to analyse processes, identify problems, test solutions and measure performance. Accurate comprehensive and timely data is very important to carry out these.

Periodic internal inspection, sentinel incident analyses, patient feedback survey, poor review are some of the measures adopted as part of quality assurance.

Structure and Process are important to provide quality in health care. They must adopt standards available, depending on the size and functions of the individual hospitals. Some of the processes are detailed in the next chapters.

The health care organizations must adopt total quality management and continue quality improvement as their philosophy. As part of their quality assurance program the organizations may make use of various quality tools, quality circle, six sigma, lean or any other similar methodologies to achieve their quality goals.

Credentialing and Privileging

Credentialing is the process of obtaining, verifying and assessing the qualifications of a practitioner to provide care or services in or for a health care organization. Credentials are documented evidence of licensure, education, training, experience or other qualifications.

Privileging is the process, whereby a specific scope and content of a patient care services (that is clinical privileges) are authorised for a health care practitioner by a health care organization based on evaluation of the individual's credentials and performance. A privilege is an advantage, right or benefit that is not available to everyone the rights and advantages enjoyed by a relatively small group of people, usually as a result of education and experience.

Credentialing and privileging is considered as major hospital quality assurance measure and important factor in hospital risk management.

It is done to determine appropriations for a position. Each practitioner is granted the authority to certain services to the patients in the given health care facility.

Practitioners are credentialed and privileged based on the organization policy and the regulatory norms of the profession.

This process should be carried out on all health care practitioners like doctors, nurses and technicians. Based on the credentials of education, training and experience, each staff is given privilege. The doctors, nurses are permitted to carry out the specific functions. E.g. Interventional Cardiologist can perform the procedure but not all physicians. Similarly, neonatal nursing can be performed only by those nurses who have been trained in that branch.

PROCESS OF CREDENTIALING AND PRIVILEGING

- Define the scope of services of the organizations
- The professionals required for those services
- To know the state laws and regulations which specify the
- Qualification, experience and skill.

- To define the qualification, experience and skills required for each service.
- The practitioner provides his details and submits copies of his licenses and intimates if he was convicted, penalized or has any ongoing litigation related to profession.
- The information may be verified with education institutions/ universities, training & work places, licensors.
- If needed, an interview may be held to seek clarifications.
- The report is submitted to the credentialing and privileging committee. Upon its approval, the same be communicated to the health care professional.
- The same is to be conducted periodically In between, the areas of privileges may be withdrawn or added if he is found wanting or if he has acquired additional skills or training.

Some elements required for transparent and effective credentialing and privileging process.

- The process must be thorough, fair and timely.
- It must involve unbiased and good faith review by peers within or outside the hospital as appropriate to the individual candidates.
- Credentialing process must be clearly written down to maintain transparency.
- Confidentiality and protection of information to be ensured in credentialing and peer review.
- Police and policies in the event of breach or violation of privileging.

Credentialing and privileging are seen as means that allow a hospital optimization and adequate utilization of most crucial resources, including specialist and human resource experts, which helps to provide efficient and quality patient care.

The credentialing and privileging process is vital to maintain the quality assurance among all staff especially and doctors. Regular verification of the credentials of health care practitioners and definition of their privileges are required for ensuing patient safety, reduction of medical errors, and provision of high quality health care services.

Clinical Algorithm

Clinical Algorithm is a text format that is specifically suited for presenting a sequence of clinical decisions for teaching clinical decision making and for guiding patient care.

Algorithm – It is a systematic process consisting of an ordered sequence of steps, each step depending on the outcome of the previous one.

In clinical medicine, a step by step protocol for management of a health care problem.

Medical algorithm is any computation formula statistical survey, monogram or look up table useful in health care.

Medical algorithms include decision tree approaches to health care treatment (e.g. if systems ABC are evident, use treatment X).

They are part of a broader field, which is usually fit under the aims of medical informatics and medicine decision making.

Medical decisions occur in several areas of medical activity including medical test, selection, diagnosis, therapy and prognosis and automatic control of medical equipment.

It is a map for teaching clinical decision making protocol charts for guiding step by step care of specific problems.

A clinical algorithm can be written for any area of medical decision making that can be standardised.

Using them medical practice becomes more effective and it can be monitored better.

A wealth of medical information exists in the form of published medical algorithms. These algorithms range from simple calculations to complex outcome predictions. Most clinicians use only a small subset routinely.

A common class of algorithms are embedded in guidelines on the choice of treatments by national state and local healthcare organizations and provided as knowledge resource for day to day use.

The intended purpose of medical algorithms is to improve and standardize decisions made in the delivery of medical care. They assist in standardizing selection and application of regimes with algorithm automation, intended to reduce potential introduction of errors. Some attempt to predict the outcome e.g. critical care scoring.

Medical algorithms based on best practice can assist everyone involved in delivery of evidence based standardised treatment via wide range of clinical care providers. Many of them as Protocols.

A ward of caution is, when algorithms whose contents are not wholly available for scrutiny and open to improvement should be regarded with suspicion.

Computations obtained from medical algorithms should be compared with and tempered by clinical knowledge and physician judgement.

Statutory Compliance for Hospitals

One of the requirements for quality assurance is to comply with all the relevant and applicable laws in that region. There are innumerable licenses, approvals to be obtained and laws to be followed. They may be summarised as follows.

- Legal Entity: Every hospital has its own legal status. It may be government owned or privately owned. In the latter case it may be Proprietary concern, Partnership Company, Charitable institution or a co-operative society. Appropriate registration and licenses must be obtained and renewed periodically.
- Land Building Laws: They may be purchased, leased or rented. The relevant agreement registration papers must be obtained and preserved. Similarly, occupation certificate, along with the approved drawing must be obtained from local authorities.
- Equipment: Some of the medical equipment like radiological equipment like ultra-sonography, MRI require to be registered with appropriate authorities under PCPNDT acts. Similarly, under AERB act X-Ray machine, the use of radioactive material/equipment needs to be registered and regulated.
- Fire and Explosion Prevention and Control: No objection certificate from local fire authorities after complying the norms is essential. A separate license for the use of fuel in kitchen is also necessary.
- Licence from authorities for control of explosives for storing diesel, and other fuel needs to be obtained.
- Support Services: Licenses to run a canteen, kitchen, laundry and other service are required. If they are outsourced the vendors must have license.
- Pollution Control Regulation: The hospital should get registration with the State Pollution Control Board, Air Control, Water Control and Biomedical Waste Rules must be complied. Consent to operate must be obtained after having facilities to dispose of the biomedical waste, both solid and liquid waste, as per the provisions of the rules (including STP and ETP).

Quality In Healthcare

- Hospital Functioning
- Clinical Establishment Act: or any other state law to register the organization. It needs to be obtained after fulfilling the requirements. The same is to be renewed periodically.
- Depending on the facilities and functions, the hospital should follow the provisions of the following laws.
- MTP Act: If MTP's are being carried out.
- PCPNDT Act: For using ultrasonography, Colour Doppler, MRI machines. All doctors must get themselves registered to use them.
- HOTA: If organ transplants are to be carried out all provisions to be followed including registration of doctors.
- Drugs and Cosmetic Act
- Various Licenses to be obtained. Special license for use of narcotics is required. (NDPS act is applicable)
- Blood Bank: To start and run a blood bank (whole blood and blood components) a separate licence needs to be obtained.
- Mental Health Act: If it is a psychiatric hospital or nursing home needs a separate licence. The provisions must be complied.
- AERB: To use radioactive material, and the equipment, separate licenses are required. It starts with the permission to build the facility and import the equipment. It also prescribes the qualification of the staff Radiation Safety measures come under the provision of AERB. Thus, wherever X-Rays are used likely conventional X-ray machines, CT Scans, the staff need to follow the measures.
- Birth and Death Registration Act: The provisions need to be followed by all doctors and hospitals.
- Notifiable Diseases: The hospital has to report the notifiable diseases to the authorities.
- Laws related to Human Resources: Several laws are applicable for example Child Labour (Prohibition & Regulation) Act, Employees Provident Fund Act, ESIS Act, Workmen Compensation Act, Maternity Benefit Act, Minimum Wages Act, Payment of Bonus Act, Equal Remuneration Act, Industrial Dispute Act, Protection of Human Rights. The relevant provisions must be followed by the hospitals.

- ➤ There are some other acts applicable to professionals working in hospitals. e.g., Indian Medical Council Act. Indian Nursing Council Act, Dentist Act, Apprentice Act.
- ➤ Laws related to Finance: There are several laws need to be followed. Financial Management is a challenging job in hospitals. Some charitable hospitals are eligible for some concessions and exemptions. Some of the laws Public Trust Act, Indian Contract Act, Customs Act, Foreign Exchange Management Act, IRDA Act.
- ➤ Other statistics like laws related to Information Technology Metrological Act etc.

There are so many regulations applicable to hospitals. It is mandatory to follow them to provide quality health care to the patients.

Risk Management

For want of a nail the shoe was lost, For want of the shoe the horse was lost, For want of the horse the rider was lost, For want of the rider the battle was lost, For want of battle the kingdom was lost, Kingdom was lost and all for the want of a nail.

English Proverb

Risk management in health care is potentially more important than any other industry. In most industries an organization develops and implements risk management strategies in order to prevent and mitigate financial losses. The same can be used for health care but patient safety is more vital here. Risk management in healthcare can mean the difference between life and death, which makes the stakes significantly higher.

Joint commission defines risk management in healthcare as "Clinical and administrative activities undertaken to identify, evaluate and reduce risk of injury to patients, staff and visitors and risk of loss of organization itself.

Managing risk is a proactive function. It is taking action to reduce the frequency and severity of unexpected incidents, reduce the legal claims and promote high reliability performance system design. The main aim is to prevent, or minimize faulty systems, processes and conditions that lead people to make mistakes or fail to prevent them.

TYPES OF RISKS FACED BY HOSPITALS

- Clinical Risk: Risk to the patient safety as a result of failure in the process of clinical care. Overall risk is directly proportional to the magnitude of damage and likelihood of occurrence. As the treatments are becoming more and more complicated and technically there is more and more scope for errors in both diagnosis and management.
- Financial Risk: Hospitals are largely dependent on the demand they create and retain the customer base in the healthcare market which in turn depend on the outcomes, patient satisfaction, public relation and several other factors.

There are several external agencies like Health Insurance Companies, Government schemes that dictate the proper financial planning. To avoid and manage risks is also necessary.

- Health and Safety: Health organizations should be concerned about potential failures of their systems because improving this system could avoid low probability, high consequence failures at low cost.
- Legal: Issues leading to medico legal suit or consumer litigation.
- Quality and Performance: Any event leading to a compromise on the quality of care.
- Reputation: Loss of reputation is significant in reducing the patient confidence and eventually affecting the attendance, occupancy and revenue. Media plays a major role in building or damaging the reputation.
- Customer related risks: Verbal or physical abuse by patients and relatives, damage to the property, violence and vandalism are frequent threats to the hospitals.
- Data Loss: Misappropriation and manipulation of hospital records of various forms are considered as major risk. With increasing use of computerization this has passed a major risk.
- Employee related, Employee mis behaviour especially strikes are a significant part of risks to the patient care.
- Risk related to noncompliance to statutory requirements.
- Regulatory measures related to safety environment, radiation, utility services, labour laws etc. may result as major risks if they are not complied by the hospitals.
- Risk management There should be well designed programme in the hospital. A qualified and experienced risk manager should be appointed with a team to support and assist him.

To implement a pro-active risk management strategy, simple seven step process may be followed.
- Employees Education (covering all aspects of risk management strategies including how to prevent and respond to risks).
- Accurate and complete documentation.
- Departmental co-ordination (To keep everyone on the same page which expedites the risk management process)
- Prevention (Employees to take steps to prevent what is avoidable).

- Correction (Employees react to risks that are unavoidable with great speed and accuracy).
- Complaints (To handle complaints in order to risks to organization)
- Incident reporting (to report an incident to reduce risks to the organization)

Though risk analysis is a prospective process the relevant topic for risk analysis is decided by the experience of incident reports. The incident reporting must be robust and transparent and should be designed to accomplish the tasks like

- Identifying and detecting risks
- Assigning values to the risks
- Anticipating losses
- Deciding upon objective steps to minimize the impact on patient and hospital

TOOLS FOR RISK ASSESSMENT

Quality risk management consists of three main elements

- Risk assessment - Analysis
  - Identification
  - Evaluation
- Risk Control - Reduction
  - Acceptance
- Risk Review - Review & Evaluation
- This is carried out by using risk management tools. There are tools available for this purpose
- HFMEA (Health Care Failure Mode and Effects Analysis)
- Risk Matrix
- Probability rating
- Severity Rating
- Event tree analysis and cause and effect diagram
- Swift (Structured what if technique)

HFMEA – It has been designed by the VA national centre for patient safety.

Failure mode effect is defined as varying result of failure mode

… i.e., No effect to vary damaging. The steps of HFMEA are:

- ➤ Define the topic - which should be relevant and to be selected from previous incident reports.
- ➤ Assemble the team : at the concerned and users
- ➤ Graphically described the process
- ➤ Conduct a hazard analysis
- List all possible failure modes
- Determine the severity of each effect
- Determine the potential causes
- Determine the probability of occurrence
- Develop an Action Plan
- Identify the action plan for each failure
- Identify process and outcome measures
- Identify single responsible individual by whom the plan is to be completed
- Record time frame.

Follow Up & Review

It is essential that Health care industry needs to do more research in this field and share the experience to prevent or reduce morbidity and mortality due to medical errors.

Patient Safety

"First, do no harm" is the most fundamental principle of any health care service. No one should be harmed in health care; however, there is compelling evidence of a huge burden of avoidable patient harm globally across the developed and developing health care systems. This has major human, moral, ethical and financial implications.

Patient safety is defined as "the absence of preventable harm to a patient and reduction of risk of unnecessary harm associated with health care to an acceptable minimum." Within the broader health system context, it is "a framework of organized activities that creates cultures, processes, procedures, behaviours, technologies and environments in health care that consistently and sustainably lower risks, reduce the occurrence of avoidable harm, make error less likely and reduce impact of harm when it does occur."Patient Safety is the key component of quality and an integral part of the health care systems. It means avoidance, prevention, and amelioration of adverse events and injuries arising from or during the processes of health care. In developed countries, 1 in 10 patients experiences adverse events and harm in hospitalized care settings. Available evidence reflects that 15% of hospital expenditure takes place in addressing the issue related to safety failures.

Patient safety is a new healthcare discipline that emphasizes the prevention reducing, reporting and analysis of medical error that often leads to adverse health care events.

Quality health care is an over reaching umbrella under which patient safety resides.

Institute of Medicine (ICM) considers patient safety "indistinguishable from the delivery of quality health care".

It also defines – "Patient Safety as Prevention of harm to patients". Emphasis is placed on the system of care delivery that

1. Prevents errors
2. Learns from errors
3. Built on a culture of safety that involves health care professionals, organizations and patients.

AHRQ Patient Safety Network Website expands upon the definition of prevention of harm "freedom from accidental or preventable injuries, produced by medical care".

"Do no harm" is a guiding principle for all health care professionals since the time of Hippocrates.

Recognizing that health care errors impact 1:10 patients around the world, the World Health Organization calls patient safety an enduring concern.

The problem and challenge is enormous. In the United States, the full magnitude and impact of errors in health care was not appreciated until 1990's when several reports brought attention to this issue. Institute of Medicine released a report "To error is human. Building a safer health system".

It found that 44000-98000 preventable deaths occur annually due to medical errors, in hospitals, 7000 preventable deaths related to medication errors. IOM called for national effort to include establishment of Centre for Patient Safety.

Experience in other countries was no different.

> In Australia it was found that 18000 annual deaths due to medication errors.

> In UK, NHS study found that there were 8, 50,000 incidences of medical errors.

> In Canada, it was estimated that 7% of all admitted in hospitals, were affected by medical errors.

Outcomes of harm consequent to medical errors may include patient complication (including extended hospital stay or readmission, disabilities even death), adverse publicity in the media, loss of professional and institutional reputation and credibility, legal and financial liability. The impact affects all stakeholders, patients, families, staff organizations and society at large.

Common sources of patient harm

Medication errors: Medication-related harm affects 1 out of every 30 patients in health care, with more than a quarter of this harm regarded as severe or life threatening. Half of the avoidable harm in health care is related to medications.

Surgical errors: Over 300 million surgical procedures are performed each year worldwide. Despite awareness of adverse effects, surgical errors continue to occur at a high rate; 10% of preventable patient harm in health care was reported in surgical settings, with most of the resultant adverse events occurring pre- and post-surgery.

Health care-associated infections: With a global rate of 0.14% (increasing by 0.06% each year), health care-associated infections result in extended duration of hospital stays, long-standing disability, increased antimicrobial resistance, additional financial burden on patients, families and health systems, and avoidable deaths.

Sepsis: Sepsis is a serious condition that happens when the body's immune system has an extreme response to an infection. The body's reaction causes damage to its own tissues and organs. Of all sepsis cases managed in hospitals, 23.6% were found to be health care associated, and approximately 24.4% of affected patients lost their lives as a result.

Diagnostic errors: These occur in 5–20% of physician–patient encounters. According to doctor reviews, harmful diagnostic errors were found in a minimum of 0.7% of adult admissions. Most people will suffer a diagnostic error in their lifetime.

Patient falls: Patient falls are the most frequent adverse events in hospitals. Their rate of occurrence ranges from 3 to 5 per 1000 bed-days, and more than one third of these incidents result in injury, thereby reducing clinical outcomes and increasing the financial burden on systems.

Venous thromboembolism: More simply known as blood clots, venous thromboembolism is a highly burdensome and preventable cause of patient harm, which contributes to one third of the complications attributed to hospitalization.

Pressure ulcers: Pressure ulcers are injuries to the skin or soft tissue. They develop from pressure to particular parts of the body over an extended period. If not promptly managed, they can have fatal complications. Pressure ulcers affect more than 1 in 10 adult patients admitted to hospitals and, despite being highly preventable, they have a significant impact on the mental and physical health of individuals, and their quality of life.

Unsafe transfusion practices: Unnecessary transfusions and unsafe transfusion practices expose patients to the risk of serious adverse transfusion reactions and transfusion-transmissible infections. Data on adverse transfusion reactions from a group of 62 countries show an average incidence of 12.2 serious reactions per 100 000 distributed blood components.

Patient misidentification: Failure to correctly identify patients can be a root cause of many problems and has serious effects on health care provision. It can lead to catastrophic adverse effects, such as wrong-site surgery. A report of the Joint Commission published in 2018 identified 409 sentinel events of patient identification out of 3326 incidents (12.3%) between 2014 and 2017.

Unsafe injection practices: Each year, 16 billion injections are administered worldwide, and unsafe injection practices place patients and health and care workers at risk of infectious and non-infectious adverse events. Using mathematical modelling, a study estimated that, in a period of 10 years (2000–2010), 1.67 million hepatitis B virus infections, between 157 592 and 315 120 hepatitis C virus infections, and between 16 939 and 33 877 HIV infections were associated with unsafe injections.

Factors leading to patient harm

Patient harm in health care due to safety breaks is pervasive, problematic and can occur in all settings and at all levels of health care provision. There are multiple and interrelated factors that can lead to patient harm, and more than one factor is usually involved in any single patient safety incident:

1. System and organizational factors: the complexity of medical interventions, inadequate processes and procedures, disruptions in workflow and care coordination, resource constraints, inadequate staffing and competency development.

2. Technological factors: issues related to health information systems, such as problems with electronic health records or medication administration systems, and misuse of technology.

3. Human factors and behaviour: communication breakdown among health care workers, within health care teams, and with patients and their families, ineffective teamwork, fatigue, burnout, and cognitive bias.

4. Patient-related factors: limited health literacy, lack of engagement and non-adherence to treatment and

5. External factors: absence of policies, inconsistent regulations, economic and financial pressures, and challenges related to natural environment.

Human factors play major role in medical errors. Most of them are preventable. Some of the examples are

Quality In Healthcare

- Medication Related: e.g. Incorrect drug, prescribed /dispensed / administered or wrong dose route, or wrong patient.
- Infection: Some of the hospital acquired infections are preventable by correct practices of cleaning disinfection or sterilization and appropriate use of antibiotics.
- Incorrect Monitoring of Patients like delay in detecting a problem, incorrect interpretation of tests, delayed referral or delayed response
- Others like patient falls, bed sores, Patient Identification errors, retained foreign objects, Complications due to incorrect techniques, failure of equipment, insufficient or continued staff resulting in errors.

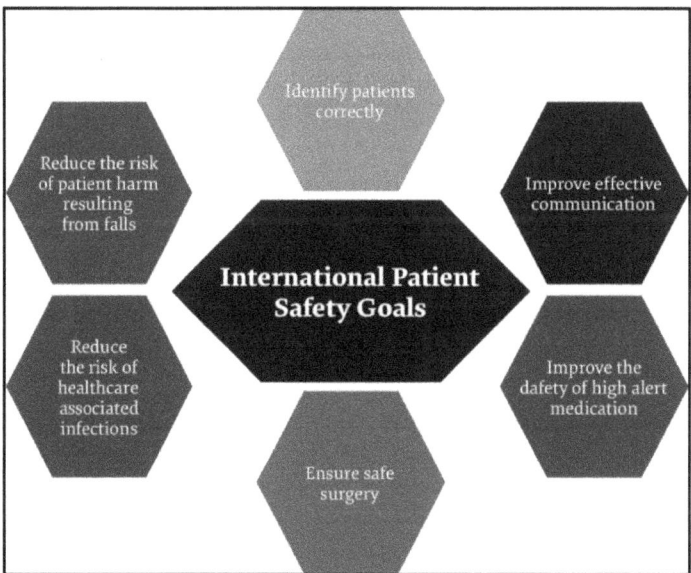

Impact: There are several terms that are used in Patient Safety and they include the levels of harm. E.g.

- Adverse Event: This event is a type of medical complication that has occurred as a result of medical care.
- Near Miss: This aims to identify a failure in a process or action that may have led to harm but was identified and stopped.
- No harm: Error happened but there was no harm.
- Adverse Drug Event: Caused by an error in prescribing dispensing transcribing or administration of medication.

> Sentinel Event: They are adverse events that lead to serious harm or death, and events that are considered unacceptable e.g. On operation on the wrong patient or part of the body, use of wrong device, patient suicide, medication errors, criminal events as rape or assault. They must be reported, and appropriate remedial action taken.

System approach to patient safety

Most of the mistakes that lead to harm do not occur as a result of the practices of one or a group of health and care workers but are rather due to system or process failures that lead these health and care workers to make mistakes.

Understanding the underlying causes of errors in medical care thus requires shifting from the traditional blaming approach to a more system-based thinking. In this, errors are attributed to poorly designed system structures and processes, and the human nature of all those working in health care facilities under a considerable amount of stress in complex and quickly changing environments is recognized. This is done without overlooking negligence or misbehaviour from those providing care that leads to substandard medical management.

A safe health system is one that adopts all necessary measures to avoid and reduce harm through organized activities, including:

- Ensuring leadership commitment to safety and creation of a culture whereby safety is prioritized.
- Ensuring a safe working environment and the safety of procedures and clinical processes.
- Building competencies of health and care workers and improving teamwork and communication.
- Engaging patients and families in policy development, research and shared decision-making.
- Establishing systems for patient safety incident reporting for learning and continuous improvement.

Investing in patient safety positively impacts health outcomes, reduces costs related to patient harm, improves system efficiency, and helps in reassuring communities and restoring their trust in health care systems.

Ensuring Patient Safety

- Leadership Commitment: Patient Safety should be care commitment. They may include it in vision or mission of the organization. Budgets, resources, training, performance review, design of infrastructure should include patient safety aspects.
- Patient Safety Committee: A patient safety committee should be set up with multidisciplinary leadership representation such as Surgeons, Physicians, Obstetricians, Intensivist, Radiologist, and Pathologist, Nursing in charge, Quality, Engineering, Pharmacy and Security Representation.

Some of its functions are

- To ensure development and approval of organization's policies and procedures related to patients' safety.
- To give directions and periodically review training of the staff related to Patient Safety.
- To carry out patient safety audit periodically.
- To evaluate reports from incident reports, complaints, audits

and other sources.

- In case of sentinel events, intensive investigation analysis and corrective measures to be undertaken.

CAUSES OF HEALTHCARE ERROR

A. Human Factors
- Variations in healthcare provider trainings, experience, fatigue, depression and burn out.
- Diverse patients' unfamiliar settings, time pressures.
- Failure to acknowledge the prevalence and seriousness of medical errors
- Increasing working hours of staff, especially nurses.

B. Medical Complexity
- Complicated technologies, powerful drugs
- Intensive care, prolonged hospital stay.

C. System Failure
- Poor Communication, unclear lines of authority of physicians, nurses and other care providers.
- Complications increase as patient to staff (especially nurses) increases.
- Disconnected reporting system within a hospital fragmented system in which numerous – handoffs of patients result in lack of co-ordination and errors.
- Drug names that alike or sound alike
- The impression that action is being taken by other groups within the institution.
- Reliance on automated systems to prevent error.
- Inadequate systems to share information about errors hamper analysis of contributory causes and improvement strategic.
- Cost-cutting measures by hospitals in response to reimbursement cutbacks.
- Environment and design factors. In emergency patient care may be rendered in areas poorly suited for safe monitoring.
- Health care, Architects have observed that many health care facilities have poor designs and safety systems.
- Infrastructure failure: According WHO 50% of medical equipment in developing countries is only partly usable due to lack of skilled operators or parts. As a result, diagnostic procedures or treatments cannot be performed leading to substandard treatment.

As per Joint Commission report on Quality
- Inadequate communication between healthcare providers, or between providers and the patient and family members was the root cause of over half the serious adverse events, in accredited hospitals.
- Inadequate assessment of the patient condition and poor leadership or training

SYSTEMS APPROACH: It is essential to institutionalize standards and protocols across the organization. A system approach rather than a person approach is required. This will reduce deviations and bring in controls.

EVIDENCE: Training of all the staff with special emphasis on patient's safety is very vital. This should be periodically conducted by modifying the contents and the methods if necessary to improve the outcome.

USE OF CHECKLISTS

A checklist will assist a person or a team to verify that a key action has been taken and remove the risk of missing a step in the process which can be a result of the complexity of work, overwork, or lapse of memory. Check list should not be mechanically or for the sake of documentation. Everybody must be trained to use them, emphasising its utility.

Infection Control

"Do no harm" is the primary objective of any health care worker. To provide safety to patients is a major challenge. To monitor the process of infection and the incidence of infection rates at different areas is a major activity in providing the quality health care.

Infection control is the discipline concerned with preventing nosocomial or health care associated infection. The common terms Infection Prevention and Control is a better term because prevention is quite important.

The measures aim to ensure the protection of those, who might be vulnerable to acquiring an infection, while receiving or rendering healthcare. The basic principle of infection prevention and control is hygiene.

Infection prevention and control address the factors related to spread of infections within the health care setting whether patient to patient, staff to patients and patients to staff or among staff.

The measures include: -

1. Prevention/ Hand Hygiene / Washing/ Cleaning
2. Disinfection/ Sterilization/ Vaccination
3. Monitoring/Surveillance/ Investigating of a

Demonstrated or Suspected spread of Infection Surveillance/Outbreak Investigation

4. Management - Interruption of outbreaks

Common Indicators

➤ Catheter Associated Urinary Tract Infection (CAUTI) Previously there was no evidence of UTI:

CAUTI = <u>Number of CAUTIs</u> x 1000 Number of Catheter days

Urinary Catheter Utilization Ratio =

<u>Number of Urinary Catheter days</u> /Number of patient days

➤ Ventilator - associated pneumonia (VAP)
➤ Hospital Acquired Pneumonia

VAP rate per 1000 ventilator days =

$$= \frac{\text{Number of VAP's}}{\text{Number of Ventilator days}} \times 1000$$

Ventilator Utilization Ratio

$$= \frac{\text{Number of Ventilator days}}{\text{Number of patient days}}$$

In a patient on mechanical ventilator support by endotracheal to be or tracheostomy for more than 48 hours

- Central Venous Catheter Blood Stream Infection (CVCBS)
- Surgical Site Infection (SSI)

$$= \frac{\text{Number of SSI}}{\text{Number of operative procedures}} \times 100$$

It may also be calculated for each specific operative procedure.

- No documented infection before surgery
- Hand Hygiene Compliance

Measured Direct observation by trend observes By Self Report

Direct Observation by patients Consumption of hygiene products Automated monitoring systems

- Infections – after procedures
- After delivery - Mother Child
- Operation Theatre - e.g., Gas gangrene
- Labour Rooms or
- Critical Care Unit Related infections

Incidence of nosocomial and other unexpected infections must be monitored in different areas of the hospital e.g. wards, maternity wing, cell paediatric ward, NICU

Central Line Associated Blood Stream Infection (CLABSI) CLABSI rate per 1000 central line days

$$= \frac{\text{Number of CLABSI}}{\text{Number of Central Line days}} \times 1000$$

Central Line Utilization ratio

$$= \frac{\text{Number of Central Line days}}{\text{Number of patient days}}$$

Medical Error

A medical error is a preventable adverse effect of care, whether or not, it is evident or harmful to the patient. This might include an inaccurate or incomplete diagnosis or treatment of a disease, injury, syndrome, behaviour, infection or other ailment.

Some of the features are described in Chapter on Patient Safety. Medical errors can be reflection of failure to provide quality health care to the patients. There may be breach in following the norms, (process) like clinical protocols or there could be some defect or depriving in providing the expected structure, medical error.

The word error in medicine is used a label for nearly all the problems having patients. Medical errors are often described as human error in healthcare. It occurs when a healthcare provider chooses an inappropriate method of care or improperly executes an appropriate method of care.

Causes of Medical Error

- Associated with inexperienced physicians, new procedures, extremes of age, complex or urgent care.
- Poor communication, improper documentation, illegible handwriting, inadequate nurse to patient ratio.
- Patients may also contribute by not following the instructions or doing something which has been prohibited.

Vast majority of medical errors result from faulty systems, and poorly designed processes. The institute of Medicine in its report. 'To err is human' which assorted that the problem in Medical Errors is not bad people in healthcare – it is the good people are working in bad systems that need to be made safer. According to WHO, 50% medical equipment in developing countries is only partly usable due to lack of skilled or parts. As a result, diagnostic procedures or treatments cannot be performed, leading to substandard treatment.

Joint commission report on Quality and Safety found that inadequate communication between healthcare providers or between providers and the patient and family members, was the root cause of over half the serious adverse events in accredited hospitals.

Poor leadership and Inadequate or improper training also contribute to medical errors risk factors include fatigue, depression

Factors related to the clinical setting include diverse patients, unfamiliar settings, and time pressures.

Medical Errors certainly signify the failure in Quality Health Care. The impact is enormous in terms of mortality (third most common cause of death in US), morbidity and financial burden.

It is essential to address all the factors to eliminate medical errors.

Medication Error

A medication error is any preventable event that may cause or lead to inappropriate medication use or patient harm while the medication is in the control of health care professional, patient or consumer.

Such events may be related to professional practice, health care products, procedures and systems including prescribing order communication product labelling, packaging and nomenclature, compounding, dispensing distribution, administration, education, monitoring and use.

A simpler definition is 'A medication is an unintended failure in the drug treatment process that leads or has the potential to lead to harm to the patient'. Mistakes can occur.

Prescribing – e.g. Incorrect drug selection (based on indications, known allergies, existing drug therapy and other factors) Dose, dosage form, quantity, route, concentration, rate of administration or instructions for use of a drug product or ordered or authorised by physician (or another legitimate prescriber).

Illegible prescriptions or medication orders that lead to error that reach patient.

DISPENSING
- To read the prescription incorrectly
- To dispense different medicine, dose
- Not to note allergies, drug interactions

STORING
- Medicines stored in the manner prescribed in relation to temperature light and humidity.

ADMINISTRATION
- Administration to the patient of a dose that is greater than the amount or less than the amount ordered the duplicate dose to the different patient.
- Inappropriate rate, procedure or technique

- Expired drug
- Look alike and sound alike medicines also cause medication errors
- Inappropriate behaviour of the patient May also be responsible
- The most common problem is self-medication
- Getting medicines directly from pharmacists
- Taking medicines for the complaints based on previous experience with the medicines

PHARMACOVIGILANCE
- Recording
- Coding
- Reporting of medical errors

Assessment

Medications errors are quite common and form a major component of medical errors. At least 1.5 million Americans are injured by medication error. On average every hospital patient is probably subjected to at least one medication error every day.

Most of the Medication Errors are preventable. It requires good policy systems and training of the persons involved and counselling of the patients and relatives. Prescription by using electronic means, reduce the errors substantially.

Medication errors, reflect a breach in quality health care. Appropriate measures must be taken to prevent these errors.

Patient Rights

In assessing the quality in health care increasing emphasis is being placed by accrediting agencies.

Patient rights are those basic rules of conduct between patients and medical caregivers as well as the institutions and people that support them.

A patient is anyone who has requested to be evaluated by a healthcare professional.

Medical care givers include hospitals, healthcare personnel. Legal definition of patient's rights is general statement, adopted by most healthcare professionals, covering such matters as access to health care, patient dignity confidentiality and consent to treatment.

Patient's rights have been decided by individual institutions based on their own policies. But the basic framework remains same which is based on Human Rights principle.

- ➤ Right to receive health care is a fundamental right, especially in case of emergencies.
- ➤ To receive right care at right time regardless of age, race, sex.
- ➤ Right to be treated with respect, courtesy and dignity.
- ➤ Right to choose the healthcare providers, change them, ask for second opinion.
- ➤ Based on principle of autonomy to give or refuse treatment or to discontinue treatment.

Right to health implies access to good health care which has been recognized as a fundamental right. Right treatment at right time is his right.

Right to be treated with respect, courtesy and dignity is an important right.

Autonomy of the patient is an ethical principle. Concept of informed consent of the patient for examination, diagnosis and treatment, after the doctor has explained the pros and cons is a legal right of the patient. Based on the concept of autonomy to refuse treatment, change the doctors and hospitals and discontinue treatment are also patient's rights.

Confidentiality about the health status is another right. This right also extends to patient's health records and communication. They cannot be handed over to anybody else except to the patients or to the authorized person.

To receive information about the facilitation, tariffs, rules and regulations of the health institutions is yet another right of patients.

To get copies of the medical records and different certifications are also his rights.

Rights and responsibilities are the two sides of the same coin. To enjoy rights completely patients should know and carry out their responsibilities.

Mutual trust, respect and effective communication are very essential for good patient-doctor relationship, which helps to provide best possible treatment to patients.

Responsibilities

- Patients must respect and trust their doctors. They must behave with courtesy with all the health providers.
- They must be frank and open with their doctors. Complete history, (current and past) must be told truthfully. The habits, past visits to other doctors, investigations, operations and medications must be informed without hiding anything.
- They should follow to all the instructions and adhere to the prescription. They must seek clarifications if they have not understood any of the doctor's advice.
- Patients must immediately inform about any adverse reactions or any dose/s is missed for whatever reasons.
- Patients should understand all the details about the facilities, rules and regulations and tariffs of the hospital.
- Patients must follow the rules and regulation and settle their bills promptly.

Performance Measure And Evaluation

As it was described earlier, structure and process are important. But their effectiveness, is eventually to be measured by outcomes. The main focus is the patient. The clinical outcomes must reflect in different areas of quality in health care to the patients. The administrative outcomes are also important to assess the performance of the management in those areas. Though it is assumed that if structure and process are as per the standards, the outcome is bound to be good is not always true. Several factors influence the outcome like

Patient Factors: Genetics, Socio-demographic health habits, beliefs, attitudes and preferences.

Environmental Factors: They include patient's cultural social, political, personal and physical characteristics as well as factors related the health professional himself. Apart from technical expertise, attitude, psychological frame, job satisfaction and motivation of health care providers play a major role in influencing the outcomes.

Various indicators have been suggested by different organizations. Some of them are mentioned in the following chapters. Patient satisfaction remains one of the main indicators of the quality health care. There are different indicators for various level, and branches of medical care. Some of the indicators for public health services and more detailed indicators for indoor services are detailed in the following chapters.

Structure Measurement:

Measures of structure evaluate the physical and organizational resources available to support health care delivery, the organization's capacity or potential for providing quality services. As such measures of structure are indirect measures of performance.

Process Measurement:

Measures of process evaluate, whether activities performed during the delivery of healthcare services are delivered satisfactorily about performance at all levels in the organization.

However good performance does not automatically translate into good results. For this another dimension of healthcare quality- outcome must be measured.

Outcome Measurement:

Measures of outcome evaluate the results of healthcare services the effects of structure and process. A common outcome measure is patient satisfaction, an indicator of how well a healthcare facility is meeting customer expectation. Other measures are mortality and complication (morbidity) rates, to identify opportunities for important average length of stay and average cost of treatment are two examples of outcome measures that examine the use of services.

Health Quality Indicators

There are several institutions accrediting bodies, journals and reports which have developed indicators to assess the quality in hospitals. Some of them are as follows

- ➢ AHRQ (75 indicators) – Agency for Healthcare Research and Quality.

They are organized into four modules

- Preventive Quality Indicators (PQI's)
- They identify hospital admissions that evidence suggests could have been avoided at least in part, through high quality outpatient care.
- Inpatient quality Indicators (IQI's) reflect quality of care inside hospitals
- Patient Safety Indicators (PSI's)
- They focus on potentially avoidable completions and iatrogenic events when patient is taking treatment in the hospitals.
- Pediatric Quality Indicators (PDI's)
- They reflect quality of care inside hospitals and identify potentially avoidable hospitalizations among children.

- ➢ The Australian Council on Healthcare Standards and Health Care Services Research Group University of New Castle (345 Indicators).

It is a Clinical Indicator Program (CIP) examines data sourced from a broad range of clinical specialty areas. It includes Clinical Indicators that are relevant to inpatient, outpatient and community health facilities which were developed by specialist clinicians.

- ➢ National Health Services Choices Hospital Score Card:

The NHS has developed a score card in which hospitals are assessed and compared in a variety of areas depending on the treatment/condition a patient is interested in areas are

- Wait time from referral to treatment
- Length of stay in hospital
- Risk of readmission (Rated lower than expected and higher
- than expected).
- Patient experiences during treatment (respect, dignity and feeling involved).
- Survival rate for elective procedure (rated better than, worse than or as expected).
- Survival rate for emergency procedure
- MRSA control for elective patients
- Cleanliness of hospital

It defines five key areas for assessment

- Clinical Effectiveness and Safely
- Patient Centeredness
- Production Efficiency
- Staff Orientation
- Response governance

JCI – Joint Commission International (JCI) accreditation is considered the gold standard in global health care. It identifies measures and shares best practices in quality and patient safety with the world.

NABH – National Accreditation Board for Hospitals and Healthcare Providers

It is a constraint board of Quality Council of India, set up to establish and operate accreditation programme for healthcare organizations. It has 10 chapters, 100 standards, 503 objective elements.

Each institution should decide the number of indicators – depending on the size, type and specialties in the hospital.

One such example is given below as illustration

General Indicators   - Human Resource

Finance Operational Safety

Material Management

Infection Control

Pharmacy and Medical Store Medical Record Maintenance and Reporting Indicators

Discharge Indicators

Diagnostic Indicators -   Internal Medicine

Paediatrics

Gynecology and Obstetrics Orthopedics

Neurology

Nephrology Oncology Cardiology Psychiatry

Examples of some simple indicators

A. General

Doctor: Bed Ratio

Nurse to Bed Ratio

Doctor to ICU Patient Ratio   Nurse to patient ratio

Bed occupancy ratio

Percentage of LAMA patients Average Admission Time Average Discharge Time

Average Length of stay (ALOS) Medical

Average Length of Stay (ALOS) Surgical STAT test turn around

Section rate Time in ration to normal deliveries

B. Fire Safety Measures
   i. Fire Extinguishers per unit of functional area. NOC from Fire Department
   ii. Documented Infection Control Procedures

C. Surgical Site Infection Rates
- VAP - ICU Ventilator Associated Pneumonia Availability of Surveillance Records of Hospital Acquired Infections (Urinary Tract Infection)
- Catheter Related UTI rate in both ICU and wards

- Incidence of Needle Stick injuries who received Post Exposure Prophylaxis (PEP) as per standard protocol
- Post-Operative Complication rate
- Adverse Event Rate
- Mortality Rate - General
- ICUs
- Post-Operative
- Neonatal

Patient Assessment As Per Joint Commission On Accreditation Oof Healthcare Organisation (JCAHO)

World Health Organization

Performance Assessment Tool for Quality Improvement in Hospitals (PATH)

JCAHO requires the tracking of the following.

- ➤ Staff qualification and experience.
- ➤ Quantity and quality of staff (ratios)
- ➤ Quantity and quality of facilities (physical layout, equipment).
- ➤ Management's commitment to quality management and improvement

- **Service Quality Indicators –**
  - ➤ Convenience (living arrangement)
  - ➤ Speed of services (waiting time, lag time, down time)
  - ➤ Friendliness.
  - ➤ Courtesy of staff

- **Appropriateness Indicators –**
  - ➤ Providing only necessary care. (caesarean section rates, hysterectomy rates, angioplasty)
  - ➤ Cost efficiency measures.
  - ➤ ALOS (Average Length of Stay)

- **Basic Clinical Indicators – ('negative measures')**
  - ➤ Death rates
  - ➤ Major complications

(Need for diagnostic related groups and severity adjusted data.)

- **Sophisticated Clinical Indicators –**
  - ➤ Unscheduled return to the emergency department within 72 hours (increased infection rate with increased LOS: low LOS with high readmission rate)
  - ➤ Infection rates.
  - Functional Status Indicators – Emotional and physical status prior to and after surgery.

- **Access Indicators –**
  - CONTINUOUS QUALITY IMPROVEMENT - Certain Other Indicators of Quality (also indicators for cost- efficiency in hospitals)
  - ➤ Length of stay.
  - ➤ Caesarean section rates.
  - ➤ Readmission rates.
  - ➤ Infection rates.
  - ➤ Adverse drug reactions.
  - ➤ Unplanned returns to surgery.
  - ➤ Unplanned admission to special units.

Patient Satisfaction

Patient satisfaction is an important and commonly used indicator for measuring quality in health care.

It is a measure of the extent to which a patient is content with the health care, which they received from their health care provider. In evaluations of health care quality, patient satisfaction is a performance indicator.

Patient satisfaction affects clinical outcomes patient retention and malpractice claims. It affects the timely efficient and patient centred delivery of quality healthcare. Patient satisfaction is thus a proxy, but a reasonably effective indicator to measure the success of healthcare providers and the healthcare organization.

Patient satisfaction is mainly dependent on the duration and efficiency of care, and how empathetic and communicative the health care providers are. It is favoured by a good-doctor patient relationship. Also, patients who are well informed of the necessary procedures in a clinical encounter and the time it is expected to take are generally more satisfied even if there is a longer waiting time. Another critical factor influencing patient satisfaction is the job satisfaction experienced by the care provider.

Patients' satisfaction is important because there are several benefits to all stake holders if patient is satisfied.

- Patient satisfaction leads customer (patient) loyalty
- Improved patient retention. According to one study, if one customer is satisfied, information reaches four others, but if
- one customer is dissatisfied, it spreads to ten or more (if the problem is serious)
- Satisfied loyal patients are not affected by higher prices nor do they go on comparing the prices. In a study it was found that 70% of patients were willing to pay more if they had to consult a quality physician.
- Profitability: To maintain profitability, patient's satisfaction is very important. In USA in one study it was estimated that due to dissatisfaction of patients, there was loss of $2, 00,000 in income over the lifetime of practice.

- Increased staff morale with reduced staff turnover also leads to increased productivity.
- Reduced risk of malpractice suits. An inverse correlation has been reported for patient satisfaction rates and medical malpractice suits.
- Accreditation Issues: Various accreditation agencies like International Organization for Standards, Joint Commission on Accreditation of Healthcare Organization, National Accreditation Board of Hospitals etc. all focus on quality service issue.
- Increased personal and professional satisfaction

RELATION BETWEEN PATIENT SATISFACTION AND QUALITY OF HEALTHCARE

It is true that patient satisfaction is a good indicator of quality of healthcare. However, it is not always the case.

Patients may be dissatisfied with health care which improves their health or satisfied with health care, which does not. Latter is true in India with many unqualified doctors who are excellent in communication and are good at it.

There are several factors that influence patient's satisfaction. It depends on duration and efficiency of care and how empathetic and communicative are the health care providers. It is favoured by good doctor-patient relationship. Also, patients who are well informed of the necessary procedures in a clinical encounter and the time it is expected to take, are generally more satisfied even if there is long terms treatment. Another central factor that influences the patient satisfaction is the job satisfaction of the care providers. Thus, good communication, empathy and transparency play a major role.

METHODS OF FINDING OUT PATIENT SATISFACTION

There are different methods of assessing the patient satisfaction. It may be

- Internal – i.e. from the staff of the hospital when patient is availing services.
- By external agencies – the latter is perhaps more accurate and objective as patients are more frank and forthcoming. Obviously

this method costs money. In the US more than 50% of the hospitals adopt this method

Survey can be by

- Interviews
- By asking patients to fill the pre-determined forms

They can also be

- Structured
- Open

The structured forms are more useful as they cover all aspects of services the management wants to assess. Personal interview has the advantage of explaining and seeking clarification from the patients but has the disadvantage of subjective elements creeping in the survey and patient may not be that open.

Some institutions follow the method of asking patients to place their feedback in a closed fashion, so that operative staff do not influence. Alternatively, some modern hospitals ask the patients to directly after feedback through computers or laptops which are received by the management.

Some feedback formats are designed to rate the services in predetermined gradation e.g. Grade 1-5 (Ascending order of satisfaction) or Unsatisfactory – to Excellent. Some questions are Yes or No. Some questions provide blank page – to be answered by the patient.

Feedbacks are taken on various aspects of the services, like outpatient, indoor, surgery diagnostic or rehabilitation care. Some may be on waiting period, some on staff response and some other on staff behaviour. It may also include feedback on various facilities and other services like diet, pharmacy and other departments. There may also be columns on suggestions for improvement.

Assessment Of Public Health Care

It is a challenge to assess the quality because of wide variations in location, infrastructure, and type of health care.

While assessing the quality it is essential to note the following in relation to public health care.

- Goals and objectives
  - Structure   -   Physical   -   Comparing
                    Facilities   with
                    Staff   Standards

- Process   -   Well defined operating procedures
                Systems
                Training
                Management Information
                System – Monitoring and Corrective action

Outcome in relation to health are indicators.

Health indicators are quantifiable characteristics of a population which researchers use as supporting evidence for describing the health of population. Usually survey method is used by them.

The most common example of health indicator is life expectancy.
CHARACTERISTICS

- Must be defined in such a way that it is measured uniformly
- Should have statistical validity
- Data collection should be feasible
- Data must have practical applications

List Of Health Indicators
Mortality Indicators
- Crude Death Rate

- Life Expectancy
- Infant Mortality rate
- Maternal Mortality rate
- Morbidity Indicators
- Prevalence
- Incidence
- Others

Health Status
- Low Birth weight
- Obesity
- Arthritis
- Diabetes
- Asthma
- High Blood Pressure
- Cancer Incidence
- Depression
- Hospital Visits
- Water borne and food borne diseases

Disability Indicators
- Disability adjusted life years (DALY)
- Other activities of daily living (ADL)
- Musculoskeletal disability (MSD) score

Nutritional Indicators
- Proportion of low birth weight
- Prevalence of anaemia
- Proportion of overweight individuals
- Nutritional intake assessments

Social and Mental Health Indicators
- Alcohol related indicators
- Injury rates

Health Determinant
- Smoking habits
- Alcohol Consumption habits
- Physical exercise habits
- Breast feeding

Assessment Of Indicators Of Indoor Services

This can be done in various areas. Here are some important areas. FRONT OFFICE

OUTCOME MEASURES
- Quality of Interaction with front office staff
- Politeness, sympathetic and helpful attitude
- Promptness of response, completeness and clarity
- Waiting period of response
- Completeness of documents
- Arrangement for waiting and interaction

EVALUATION OF QUALITY OF SERVICES
- Level of patient/public satisfaction as revealed by satisfaction surveys, complaints from patients/public/physicians.
- Average time taken in completing the admission documentation
- Average time spend by patient in queue for registration
- Level of staff satisfaction and morale of staff in the department
- Time taken for discharge – because of process and delay in billing

OUT PATIENT DEPARTMENT
- Evaluation of Quality of services
- Patient satisfaction surveys
- Complaints/suggestions received
- Monitoring of entry to exit time
- Registration
- Waiting for consultation
- Consultation time

Quality In Healthcare

- Time taken for investigation
- Time for treatment including issue of medicine
- Improvement in Health Status
- Monitoring – OPD Work Load - Overall Speciality wise Doctor wise

Emergency Services

- Response time for dispatch of ambulance when asked for
- Response time of the consultant, time taken for investigations and starting treatment
- Patients successfully resuscitated especially those requiring immediate resuscitation
- Patient care outcome – extent to which the patient's condition improved
- Death Rate in Emergency department
- Satisfaction level of patients/visitors/relatives about the care provided, ascertained from written comments, complaints, surveys.
- Number of court cases
- Daily attendance in the emergency and percentage of cases admitted.

PATHOLOGY AND LABORATORY

- Validation of test / results by outside referral laboratories.
- Internal Quality Control
- Complaints / comments from the hospital, physicians about accuracy or timeless of lab reports
- Feedback from patients in the form of waiting period complaints / comments on the technique of sample drawing or on difference of reports from outside laboratory.
- Time taken for providing reports (Emergency & Routine).
- Instances of sampling errors such as wrong labelling, wrong container, wrong technique of collecting sample.

- Validation of results by outcome of patient care because that indirectly depends on the tests from the lab.

RADIOLOGY DEPARTMENT

- Number of complaints received from patients.
- Instances of violation of PNDT /other regulations
- Film wastage rate of conventional film processing system (Not more than 10%)
- Deficiencies detected by Medical Audit committee showing lack of correlation between the radiology report and the final diagnosis / tissue reports.
- Waiting period for CPD patients.
- Frequency of investigations postponed / cancelled due to non-availability of the radiologists' equipment breakdown or power failure.
- Response time in emergency cases during non-working hours
- Time taken in generating and communicating the reports.
- Instances of breach of radiation safety norms
- Utilization pattern of equipment
- Instances of breakdown repairs and downtime

OPERATION THEATRES

- Post- operative infection rate
- Swabs for culture to check the bacterial growth
- Number of deaths on the operation table
- Number of post-operative deaths
- Surgery wise average time taken
- Cases of negligence
- OT utilization pattern including the idle time
- Instances of tissue report differing from the operative findings and surgery conducted by the surgeon
- Adverse / sentinel / near miss events

BLOOD BANK
- Number of outdated / wasted units
- Gross Match: Transfusion ratio Should not be more than 1:5:1
- Incidence of Transfusion Reactions
- Number of surgical procedures postponed /cancelled due to non-availability of blood
- Number of emergency requisitions received and met, and average time taken
- Number of blood units transfused per bid in a year
- Number of catalogues transfusions given
- Number of patients given the whole blood Vs. given packed cells.
- Maximum stock stored vs. storage capacity
- Total number of units received, processed issued in a year
- Average number of units transfused per patient.

REHABILITATION SERVICES
- Level of Satisfaction of patients as assessed from the regular satisfaction surveys /complaints received.
- Satisfaction of treating physicians with the results of therapy
- Instances of violation of patients' privacy / code of ethics
- Incidence of burns / other complications (due to negligence of staff)

MATERNITY SERVICES
- Caesarean Section rate
- Material death rate
- Perinatal Mortality
- Instances of maternal / foetal deaths due to mismanagement of labour at any stage
- Incidence of unexpected complications such as burst uterus foetal distress post-mortem haemorrhage hyper bilirubin a cerebral haemorrhage

Quality In Healthcare

- Instances of avoidable complications / permanent damage to the baby as birth trauma, cerebral anoxia, retrolental fibroplastia infection, hypoglycaemia or hypthorinia.
- Incidence of theft and swapping of babies. INPATIENT WARDS
- Level of patient satisfaction with the services provided as assessed from
- A system of written feedback, obtained as per the structured format at the time of discharge.
- Complaints from doctors on any aspect of ward management
- Incidence of medication errors in the ward
- Incidence of nosocomial infections in the ward
- Incidences of any harm to the patient because of negligence in performance of duty by the nursing staff such as bed sores, hot water burns, etc.
- Complaints of Impolite / rude behaviour of nursing / other staff.
- Incidence of delay in discharge due to delay in preparation of discharge documents and process
- Number of complaints about food supplied due to lapses on the part of ward staff
- Deficiencies in patient's medical records as pointed out by the medical / nursing audit committee.
- Incidence of violation of patient's privacy by the staff / visitors.
- Incidence of compromise of patients' security such as assault, theft and molestation and rape in the ward.
- Incidence of fire / other hazards
- Response time of nurses / doctors / other staff

CRITICAL CARE UNITS (CCU) INDICATORS

- Incidence of Bed sores
- Incidence of Nosocomial infection
- Incidence of Complications (especially unexpected)
- Net Death rate in Critical Care cases
- Consultants' response time

- Satisfaction level of patients (consultants, residents, nurses,
- technicians, housekeeping staff)
- Incidence of adverse/sentinel near miss events.
- NEONATAL INTENSIVE CARE UNIT (NICU)
- Neonatal mortality rate
- Neonatal survival rate
- Cases of HAI in NICU
- Cases of avoidable complications / death
- Observations by Medical Audit and Nursing Audit Committee
- Level of satisfaction of relative as ascertained from satisfaction survey / complaints received.
- Incidence of adverse / sentinel/ near miss events

DIALYSIS SERVICES

- Level of satisfaction of patient as well as attendants with the dialysis arrangement and benefits to the patient.
- Incidence of complications during dialysis
- Incidence of post dialysis side effects such as anaemia,
- nutritional deficiencies
- Incidence of cross infection
- Percentage of patients, who received adequate dialysis
- treatment, as verified by reduction in the level of urea
- creatinine (up to 65%) and body weight
- Patients survival rate – (it may be up to 20% mortality in some centres)
- Cost of services
- Conversion of negative to positive (HbAg)

PHARMACY

- Instances of stock out of items, the time taken for replenishment and losses due to emergency purchases.
- Instances and volume of expiry date and deterioration of stocks due to improper storage
- Instances from physicians regarding the drug items being substandard / non-effective / toxic aid the action taken there off.
- Instances of issues of wrong medicines by the pharmacists
- Instances of wrong pharmacy billing /overcharging from the patients.
- Instances of drugs being issued without proper prescriptions, especially narcotic / dangerous drugs.
- Time taken at the pharmacy counter for issue of prescriptions
- Instances of violation of rules/regulations.

MEDICAL RECORDS

- Number of records found incomplete during random checks by members of the Medical Record Committee (MRC)
- Number of records found damaged during random check by the MRC
- Percentage of records found missing / untraceable during random check by MRC
- Time taken for retrieval of records.
- Complaints from patients / relatives about delay non- availability of documents.
- Complaints from health authorities about delay /non receipt of reports /returns
- Observations by the courts and insurance agencies
- Observations by the Medical Audit Committee / Nursing
- Audit Committee about the quality of records generated, preservation of records or timely availability and quality of statistics as reported by the users.
- Instances of breach of confidentiality of information

- Physical condition of records as seen during periodic inspections (Dust, fungal growth, damage by posts and seepage of water).

CSSD
- Incidence of incomplete sterilization as detected by the periodic random testing of sterilized items by culture of swabs taken.
- Incidence of incomplete sterilization as detected from the colour of test strips inside the packs
- Complaints from users / clients about incorrectness of packing / contents / damaged items packed or improper cleaning.

DIETARY DEPARTMENT
- Number of complaints received from patients / visitors and staff and the type of complaints
- Instances of food poisoning or any untoward effects on consumers
- Instances of serving wrong diets to the patients
- Wastage, theft, pilferage of food
- Instances of non-serving or serving inadequate quantity
- Pests / rodents menace as observed during inspection

LAUNDRY AND LINEN DEPARTMENT
- Patients' feedback
- Number of complaints / comments received from patients, staff about quality of linen or quality of wash
- The timeliness of linen supply
- The quality of linen supplied (worn out / faded / starved,
- patched, smelling or poorly ironed
- The quantity of linen supplied
- Average monthly cost of linen replacement
- Losses due to thefts, pilferage or damage in process

HOUSEKEEPING INDICATORS

- Visual Effect
- Comments from patients / relatives as ascertained through
- patient satisfaction survey / complaints / suggestion
- Complaints from staff (especially the doctors / nurses) in the patient care areas
- Instances of noncompliance of Biomedical Waste (BMW) management rules
- Increase / Decrease in HAI (Hospital Acquired Infections) attributable to Housekeeping services
- Extent of post / rodent nuisance as reported by dietary / other staff.

Third Party Recognition

In the past it was mentioned that ultimate recognition of quality management must be from external agencies.

- ➤ Licensing

It is compulsory. Without them the health care facilities should/cannot function. They have been detailed in earlier chapter 'Statutory Compliance'.

- ➤ Certification, Accreditation

There are several recognized organizations which carry out this

process. Though it is voluntary, some governments have made it compulsory. Policies of Health Insurance Agencies in some countries, make it almost compulsory to seek accreditation. In India too, there is a small beginning. Central government makes arrangement to treat its employees only in those hospitals which have NABH accreditation. Recently Insurance Regulatory and Development Agency (IRDA) has made it mandatory to have at least Entry level NABH accreditation to receive Cashless facility from Health Insurance Companies.

- ➤ Prizes and Awards

They are voluntary. The healthcare institutions may apply to

showcase their quality of services.

- ➤ One of the criticism against the accreditation is too much focus on documentation. In the process, the main activity i.e. patient care may suffer. Another issue is using accreditation as a marketing tool, rather than improving quality of health care.

International Standard Organisation (ISO)

ISO is an independent, non-governmental organization with a membership of 163 standard bodies. Through its members it brings together experts to share knowledge and develop voluntary, consensus based, market relevant International Standards that support innovation and provide solutions to global challenges.

International Standards give world-class specifications for products, services and systems to ensure quality, safety and efficiency.

ISO was born from union of two organizations. One was the ISA (International Federation of the National Standardizing Association) and other was UNSCC (United Nations Standards Co-ordinating Committee).

ISO began in 1946 when delegates from 25 countries met at the Institute of Engineers in London and decided to facilitate new International Organization on 1946. On 23rd January, 1947 the new organization ISO officially began its operations. Since then they have published over 21000 International Standards, covering almost all aspects of technology manufacturing and services. Its central secretariat is in Geneva Switzerland.

Because International Organization for Standardization would have different acronym, different languages it was decided to give its short form ISO – which in Greek means Equal.

ISO standards are developed by the people that need them, through a consensus process. Experts from all over the world develop the standards that are required by their sector. They reflect a wealth of international experience and knowledge.

There are several benefits of ISO International Standards. They ensure that products and services are safe, reliable and quality. For businesses, they are strategic tools that reduce costs by minimizing waste and errors and increasing productivity. They help companies to access new markets, level the playing field for developing countries and facilitate free and fair global trade.

Benefits:

Industry
- Become more competitive by offering products and services that are accepted globally.
- Enter new markets easily
- Raise profits by offering products with increased quality
- compatibility and safety
- Reduce costs by not reinventing the wheel and using available resources better benefit from the knowledge and best practice of leading experts around the world.

Regulators
- Harmonize regulations across countries to boost global trade
- Increase credibility and treat throughout the supply chain
- Make it easier for countries to outsource and specialize

Society
- Wider choice of sale and reliable products and services at competitive prices
- Best practice and concerted action at the organizational level to practically address global challenges like climate change and sustainability

The popular standards are

ISO – 9000	-	Quality Management
ISO – 14000	-	Environmental Management
ISO – 450001	-	Occupational Health and Safety
ISO /IFC 27001	-	Information Security
ISO 2600	-	Social Responsibility
ISO 50001	-	Energy Management
ISO 3166	-	Country Codes
ISO 4217	-	Currency Codes
ISO 639	-	Language Codes

ISO 22000 - Food Safety Management

ISO 20121 - Sustainable events

ISO 13485 - Medical Devices

ISO 31000 - Risk Management

ISO 37001 - Anti Bribery Management

ISO 8601   - Date and Time format

ISO 9000

ISO 9000 family addresses various aspects of quality management system and contains some of ISO's best known standards. The standards provide guidance and tools for companies and organizations who want to ensure that their products and services consistently meet customer's requirements and that quality is consistently improved.

Standards in ISO 9000 family include

- ISO 9001: 2015 - Sets out requirements of a quality management system.
- ISO 2015 – covers the basic concepts and language
- ISO 9004: 2009 – Focuses on how to make a quality
- management system more efficient and effective
- ISO 19011:2011 – Set out guidance on internal and external audits of quality management systems ISO 9001:2015

It sets out the criteria for quality management system and is the only standard in the family that can be certified. It can be used by any organization large or small, regardless of its field of activity. In fact, more than a million organization are certified to ISO – 9001.

The standard is based on a number of quality management principles including a strong customer focus, the motivation and implication of top management, the process approach and continual improvement. Using 9001:2015 helps to ensure that customers get consistent, good quality products and services which in turn brings many business benefits.

HIGH LEVEL STRUCTURE OF ISO 9001

- Scope: It specifies that the organization needs to meet customer and regulatory requirements and ensure its employees follow its policies and procedures while advancing quality through continual improvement.

- ➤ Normative references: Provides normative references those that confirm to ISO 9000's related norms to constitute the terms of ISO 9001.
- ➤ Terms and Definitions: Defines the terms used in the standard and highlights the changes from the previous ISO 9001

CONTEXT OF THE ORGANISATIONS

- ➤ Understanding the organization and its context
- ➤ Needs and expectations of the interested parties
- ➤ Determining the scope
- ➤ Management system
- ➤ Leadership
- ➤ Leadership and commitment
- ➤ Policy
- ➤ Roles, responsibility and authority
- ➤ Planning

Actions to address risks and opportunities, objectives and plans to achieve them

- ➤ Support
- ➤ Resources
- ➤ Competence
- ➤ Awareness
- ➤ Communication
- ➤ Documented Information
- ➤ Operation Operational planning and central
- ➤ Performance Evaluation
  - Monitoring, measurement, analysis and evaluation
  - Internal Audit
  - Management review
  - Improvement

- Non Conformity and corrective action
- Continual Improvement

QUALITY MANAGEMENT SYSTEM

➢ Describes the standards, the general requirements which encompass all activities from quality manual documentation and control of documents and records to determine the sequence and interaction of the processes to implementing actions to advice planned results.

➢ Management responsibility: It requires management's commitment to the organization's products, customers and planning and review processes.

➢ Resource Management: Provides the criteria needed to perform a job competency and in a safe environment. Human resources infrastructure, planning and work environment are diseases in this section.

➢ Product realization: defines the steps in product development. These steps include everything from the initial design phase to the final delivery phase. For example, product realization, planning customer related processes, design and development. The product purchasing process, production and several provisions and the control of monitoring and measuring devices.

➢ Measurement analysis and improvement: Focuses on measuring, analysing and improving the QMS by having companies perform, periodical internal audits, monitor customer's satisfaction, control non-conforming product, analyse data and take corrective and preventive action.

PRE-CERTIFICATE REQUIREMENT

➢ Organization should be deeply committed to implement ISO, quality programmes. This is especially so from the top management. It should provide all the necessary resources.

➢ It is advisable if not mandatory to appoint or assign some individual/s or agency well versed with ISO.

➢ The following documents and records required by ISO 9001: 2015.

(Some of them may not be necessary if the organization does not perform the relevant process)

A.   Documents
- Scope of the Quality Management System (QMS (clause 4.3)
- Quality Policy (Clause 5.2)
- Criteria for evaluation and selection of suppliers (clause 8.4)

B.   Records
- Monitoring and measuring equipment calibration records (Clause 7.1.5.1)
- Records of training skills experience and qualifications (17.2)
- Product/service requirements review records
- Record about design and development outputs review (clause 8.3.2)
- Records about design and developed inputs (clause 8.3.3)
- Records of design and development controls
- Records of design and development outputs (clause 8.3.4)
- Design and development changes (Clause 8.3.5)
- records (clause 8.3.6)
- Characteristics of product to be produced and service to be provided (clause 8.5.1)
- Records of customer property (clauses 8.5.6)
- Record of conformity of product/service with acceptance criteria (clause 8.6)
- Record of non-conforming outputs (clause 8.7.2)
- Monitoring and measurement results (clause 9.1.1)
- Internal audit program (clause 9.2)
- Results of Internal audits (clause 9.2)
- Results of management review (clause 9.3)
- Results of corrective actions

NON-MANDATORY DOCUMENTS

- These are most commonly used by various organizations – They are useful for implementation.
- Procedures for determining context of the organization and interested parties (clauses 4.1 and 4.2)
- Procedures for addressing risks and opportunities (clause 6.1)
- Procedures competence, training and awareness (clauses 7.1.2, 7.2, 7.3)
- Procedure for equipment maintenance and measuring equipment (clause 7.1.5)
- Procedure for document and record central (clause 7.5)
- Sales procedure (clause 8.2)
- Procedure for document and development (clause 8.3)
- Procedure for design and development (clause 8.3)
- Procedure for production and service provision (clause 8.5)
- Warehousing procedure (clause 8.5.4)
- Procedure for management of non-conformancesand corrective actions (clauses 8.7 to 10.2)
- Procedure for monitoring customer satisfaction (clause 9.1.2)
- Procedure for internal audit (clause 9.2)
- Procedure for management review (clause 9.3)

- To select an ISO certifying body, which should be based on their reputation and affordability.
- Preliminary Information about the organization is sought by the ISO certifying body.
- Once decision is made Application form is to be submitted with agreed fees.
- Then the certifying body requires the quality manual and procedures to verify that all the requirements of the standards are addressed.
- Pre assessment: Though optional it is very useful

- It is an initial review of Quality Management System to identify and significant omission or weaknesses in the system and provides the organization an opportunity to correct any deficiencies before the registration assessment is conducted, corrections and amendments are suggested.

ASSESSMENT

Flow of activities during the audit is as follows

- Opening Meeting: Introduction of audit team and keep personnel. The scope and general approach of audit is discussed.

- Brief tour of the facility

- Review of documents

- Examination: The audit is conducted, personnel are interviewed, and objective evidence is collected to show the system has been implemented.

- Daily Review: At the end of each day or beginning of the next, the audit team reviews any issues identified during the assessment. Potential findings or non-conformities may be clarified at the time.

- Closing Meeting: The audit team states their conclusions regarding the audit and presents any findings or nonconformities that were identified along with any observations they may have.

- Audit Report: Issued Audit findings may be

- Minor Non-conforming: Does not hold up the registration.

- But need to be addressed.

- Major Non-Conformance: This will hold up the registration.

Unless evidence is provided these are corrected, registration cannot be issued. Certificate is valid for three years.

POST CERTIFICATION SURVEILLANCE VISITS

(Generally, once in six months) to verify the maintenance of QMS and continued requirements

- For any non-conformation
- Suspension
- Cancellation of registration may occur
- Application for renewal to be made 3 months in advance

Joint Commission on Accreditation of Health Care Organizations (JCHAO)

In fact, Joint Commission's predecessor was an outgrowth of the efforts of Ernest Codman to reform based on outcomes management in patient care. His efforts led to the founding of American College of Surgeons Hospital Standardization Program. The present organization was established in 1951 with merger of similar organization like American college of Physicians, American Medical Association, etc.

Joint Commission advocates the use of patient safety measures, the spread of information the measurement of performance and the introduction of public policy recommendations.

Accredited organizations include:

- Ambulatory care organizations
- Assisted living facilities
- Behavioral health care organizations
- Critical access hospitals
- Clinical laboratories
- Health care networks
- Home care organizations
- Hospitals
- Long term care facilities
- Office-based surgery practices

By asking for accreditation, an organization agrees to be measured against national standards set by health care professionals. An accredited organization substantially complies with Joint Commission standards and continuously makes efforts to improve the care and services it provides.

Health care organizations seek Joint Commission accreditation because it:

- Enhances community confidence.
- Provides a report card for the public
- Offers an objective evaluation of the organization's performance.
- Stimulates the organization's quality improvement efforts.
- Aids in professional staff recruitment.
- Provides a staff education tool.
- May be used to meet certain Medicare certification requirements.
- Expedites third-party payment
- Often fulfils state licensure requirements.
- May favorably influences managed care contract decisions.

Specially trained surveyors evaluate each health care organization's compliance with Joint Commission standards and identify the organization's strengths and weaknesses. The surveyor's goal is not merely to find problems, but also to provide education land consultation so health care organizations can improve.

Application for Accreditation:

- ➤ Applicant should apply for survey by taking part in an interactive session.
- ➤ Application at least 6 months before the actual survey.
- ➤ Applicant receives Comprehensive Accreditation Manual for Health care.
- ➤ An initial survey looks at a four month track record of
- ➤ compliance with our standards.
- ➤ After the initial survey, surveyors look for a 12 month track record of compliance.

Joint Commission International (JCO)

Joint Commission (preferably JCHAO – Joint Commission on Accreditation of Healthcare Organizations) is a United States based organization that accredits more than 21,000 healthcare organizations and programs in USA. A majority of state governments recognize Joint Commission Accreditation as a condition of licensure and the receipt of Medicaid, Medicare and other health insurance reimbursements.

JCI was established in 1988 as a division of Joint Commission. Through international accreditation, consultation, publications and education programmes. JCI extends the Joint Commissions mission, worldwide by helping to improve the quality of patient care by assisting international health care organizations public. Health agencies health ministries and others evaluate, improve and demonstrate the quality of patient care and enhance patient safety in more than 60 countries.

JCI identifies measure and shares best practices in quality and patient safety. It provides leadership and innovative solutions to help healthcare organizations across all settings to improve performance and outcomes

JCI understands the local needs and diverse cultures in different countries and regions and unique patient care challenges. Yet its singular focus is on the highest patient are standards and results oriented process improvement.

JCI accredits different health care organizations like

- Hospitals
- Ambulatory care
- Clinical Laboratory
- Home Care
- Long Term Care
- Medical Transport Organizations
- Primary Care

JCI ACCREDITATION PROCESS

JCI accreditation standards for Hospitals 5th Edition provides the basis for accreditation of hospitals throughout the world, supplying organizations with information they need to pursue or maintain patient safety, performance improvement and accreditation status since April 2014 and 6th edition of standards is being published on 1st January 2017 and the effective date of these standards will be 1st July, 2017.

JCI PATHWAY TO ACCREDITATION

- START UP: To become familiar with JCI's accreditation standards and Survey process
- PLAN: To conduct gap analysis and build action plan.
- PROCESS: To update policies and procedures
- FOCUS: To target improvements where needed
- FIX BARRIERS: To work with the staff to overcome obstacles.
- READINESS: To assess the readiness at the mid - point
- TRAINING: To continue training for sustainable changes
- MONITOR AND ADJUST: Evaluate and refine processes
- MOCK SURVEY: To use mock survey to assess the readiness
- FINAL STAGE: To make final modifications

JCI STANDARDS

- Access and Continuity of Care (ACC)
- Patient and Family Rights (PFR)
- Assessment of Patients (AoP)
- Care of Patients (CCP)
- Quality and Patient Safety (QPS)
- Governance, Leadership and Direction (GLD)
- Facility Management and Safety (FMS)
- Staff Qualification and Education (SQE)
- Prevention and Control of Infection (PCI)
- Management of Information (MOI)

Getting Started for Quality

- Leadership commitment (Board Management and clinical leaders) to provide the necessary resources.
- To form a core team for planning and implementation, preferably led by a person who has the previous experience.
- To Apply to JCI
- JCI team will come over to do baseline assessment against care standards and "help us" plan. Internally:
- To do a self-assessment with internal team
- To make detailed project plan with assigned responsibilities, deliverables and time frames.
- To assign oversight of each chapter of standards to a champion/leader who will identify the team member
- To compile and prepare all the policies and procedures
- To involve physicians their commitment is vital
- To seek assistance from JCI about clarification and standards, interpretation
- To plan for a final mock survey well in advance.
- To plan final revisions and corrected on the findings of the final mock survey.
- Request on application from JCI well in advance.
- Once application is completed a surveyor team will be complied and dates confirmed.
- Team leader to co-ordinate agenda and plans for the survey
- Survey results would be conveyed.

National Accreditation Board For Hospitals And Healthcare Providers (NABH)

NABH is a constituent board of Quality Council of India, set up to establish and operate accreditation programme for healthcare organizations. It is structured to cater needs of the consumers and to set benchmarks for progress of health industry.

NABH is an institutional member as well as a board member of International Society of Quality in Health Care (ISQUA). It is also on board of Asian Society for Quality in Healthcare (ASQUA).

SCOPE OF NABH / OBJECTIVES

- Accreditation of Health Care facilities – like hospitals, SHCO, Blood Bank, Blood Storage Centre, Dental Facilities /clinics, OST centre, Allopathic Clinics, Ayush Hospitals, CHC, PHC, Wellness Centres, Clinical Trial.
- Quality Promotion, initiates like Safe I Nursing Excellence, Laboratory Certification Programs
- IEC activities, public lecture, advertisement, Workshops / Seminars
- Educators and Training for Quality and Patient safety
- Recognition: Endorsement of various healthcare quality courses/workshops
- The board consist of representatives of various healthcare stakeholders
- It has various committees like Accreditation, Technical, Assessor Management, Research and Appeals Committees'

NABH ACCREDITATION DOCUMENTS FOR HOSPITAL

Hospital Manual

It should include vision, mission and hospital quality policy, organization structure and macro-level system for compliance of hospital accreditation standard.

- Department wise manuals. e.g.

- Infection control
- Emergency Preparedness
- Medical Record
- Human Resource
- Central Sterility supply department
- Bio-medical manual
- System Procedures: To prepare system procedures to standardize the working in the hospitals and establish system approach
- Health and Safety Procedures
- Process approach for hospital: To prepare
- Standard Operating Procedures: Work Instructions and SOP's for establishing good hospital management system.
- Forms and Templates: To be prepared and filled
- Hospital Committee Books: Detailing the constitution roles and responsibilities
- NABH audit check list: To be prepared.

STEPS

Commitment from the top
- Provide resources
- Obtain standards and list of documents
- To form a strong committee and task force for documentation
- Identify and define process approach
- Define Accreditation Policy and establish objectives
- Prepare documents of Quality Management system as well as patient care and hygiene control, infection control as well as hand books
- Implementation and train personnel in the use of procedures and formats
- Self-assessment of the system
- Assign internal auditors

- Carry out Internal Audit
- Take corrective actions for non-conformance
- To conduct Management Review Meeting
- Apply for NABH accreditations
- Pre-certification assessment by NABH
- Corrective actions on suggestions by NABH auditors
- Final Audit by NABH auditors
- To submit the corrective actions for the findings of Final Audit of the Assessors
- Get accredited by NABH
- Surveillance
- Renewal.

STANDARDS AND OBJECTIVE ELEMENTS

A standard is a statement that defines the structures and processes that must be substantially in place in an organization to enhance the quality of care.

Objective element is a measurable component of a standard Acceptable compliance with objective elements determines the overall compliance with a standard.   **SECTION I**

CHAPTERS	PATIENT CENTERED STANDARDS	STD	OE
1	Access, Assessment and Continuity of Care (AAC)	15	78
2	Patients' Rights and Education (PRE)	5	29
3	Care of Patients (CoP)	18	105
4	Management of Medications (MoM)	13	61

5	Hospital Infection Control (HIC)		
SECTION II			
HEALTHCARE ORGANISATION			
MANAGEMENT STANDARDS			
CHAPTERS	**PATIENT CENTERED STANDARDS**	**STD**	**OE**
6	Continuous Quality Improvement (CQI)	6	37
7	Responsibilities of Management (RoM)	5	20
8	Facility Management and Safety (FMS)	9	41
9	Human Resource Management (HRM)	13	47
10	Information Management System (IMS)	7	41
		100	**503**

NABH - Pre Accreditation Entry Level Certification

A large number of hospitals and Health Care Organizations (HCO's) face challenges and difficulties in implementing all the Accreditation Standards of NABH. In order to facilitate gradual up-gradation, NABH has developed Pre-Accreditation Entry

Level Certification Standards in consultation with various stakeholders as a stepping stone for enhancing the quality of patient care and safety. The aim is to introduce quality and accreditation to HCO's as their first step towards awareness and capacity building.

Recently, IRDA has come with a circular that to get Cashless Services every HCO must have at least entry level certificate in next one year. So, there is renewal interest in Entry Level Certification among smaller hospitals and nursing homes.

Once Pre-accreditation Entry Level Certificate is achieved, the HCO can then prepare and move to the next progressive level(s) - and finally to Full Accreditation status.

This methodology provides a step by step and staged approach which is practical for the HCO's. The applicant HCO must have conducted self-assessment against NABH Pre entry level standards often implementing it for at least 3 months before submission of application and must ensure that it complies with the standards.

National Accreditation Board for Testing and Calibration (NABL)

NABL is a society, which provides accreditation recognition of the technical competence of a testing, calibration or medical laboratory for a specific task following ISO/IEC 17025.2005

ISO 15159/2007 standards

It is associated with Asia Pacific Laboratory Accreditation Corporation (APLAC), Mutual Recognition Arrangement (MRA), and International Laboratory Accreditation (ILAC).

NABL carries out Accreditation of the following

- Testing Laboratories : Biological Chemical Electrical Electronics, Fluid-Flow, Mechanical Non-Destructive Photometry Radiological Thermal
- Calibration Laboratory: Electro-Technical, Mechanical Fluid Flow, Thermal and Optical, Radiological.
- Medical Laboratories: Clinical Biochemistry, Clinical Pathology, Haematology and Immuno-Haematology, Microbiology and Serology, Histopathology, Cytopathology Genetics, Nuclear Medicine (in vitro tests only).

It also conducts Training Courses.

1. ISO/IEC 17025 Assessors' Training Course
2. ISO 15189 Assessors' Training Course

Procedure

- Commitment from the top to provide resources
- To procure NABL documents
- To get fully acquainted with NABL document
- To identify and appoint a person/s and train him / them in
- Quality Management System and Internal Audit
- To prepare Quality Manuals

- ➤ Ensure effective environmental condition (Temperature
- ➤ humidity, storage placement, etc.)
- ➤ Ensure calibration of instruments and equipment (Only NABL Accredited Calibration Laboratories are authorised)
- ➤ Impart Training in documents and procedures
- ➤ To incorporate Internal Quality Control
- ➤ To participate in External Quality Assessment Scheme (EQAS)
- ➤ To conduct Internal Audit and Management Review
- ➤ Once prepared, to apply for NABL with appropriate fee.
- ➤ Documents to be submitted
- ➤ Pre-assessment of the laboratory to be done by Lead
- ➤ Assessor/s
- ➤ Suggestions for modifications & corrections
- ➤ Final Assessment.

If satisfactory, Certification - valid for 3 years - will be given.

Surveillance will be carried in this period. These feedbacks are analysed by the designated officials and necessary corrective and improvement steps are taken wherever possible and necessary.

BENEFITS OF NABL ACCREDITATION

For hospitals and clinical laboratories – since the accreditation is as per the International Standards, the credibility of the results is assured all over the world. This is a great benefit to the clinicians and patients in diagnosis and management of illnesses.

ISQUA

ISQUA is the International Society for Quality in Healthcare. It is a global organization. It started in 1985.

Its Mission is "To inspire and drive improvement in the quality and safety of healthcare worldwide through education and knowledge, sharing external evaluation supporting health systems and connecting through global networks".

It has a network that spans 100 countries and five continents. Any individual or institution may join its network. It helps to achieve their healthcare goals - be it as a clinician, manager, policymaker, academic or other, in the areas of quality and safety. One of its key partners is WHO (World Health Organization). It assists WHO with technical and policy advice, as well as knowledge sharing as part of WHO initiative.

ISQUA professional development education programme, includes talk's, debates, online workshops, and web mails in all areas of health care safety and quality and fellowship programme.

ISQUA – develops ideas and solutions and exchange it through its extensive network. It covers the entire continuous of care, ranging from systems and processes to quality of patient care and performance. It also includes patients and their loved ones, who are valuable resources, as it seeks to achieve the goal of excellence in health care are delivery and outcomes.

ISQUA is involved in the accreditation of natural and regional healthcare facilities worldwide via its International Accreditation Programme. They take responsibility for assessing the standards of organization who set the benchmarks in healthcare safety and quality.

ISQUA is an essential resource for policy makers, leading patient agencies, health care workers and other health professionals around the world.

Clinical Audit

- Measurable Patient Safety
- Patient Satisfaction Patients & Responsibilities

- Legal Compliances in Hospitals
- Clinical Algorithm Credentials
- Risk Management
- Failure of Quality
- in Healthcare Case studies

CAP

(College of American Pathologists)

College of American Pathologists (CAP) -leading organization of board-certified pathologists, severe patients' pathologists and the public by fostering and advocating excellence in the practice of pathology and laboratory medicine worldwide.

The college of American Pathologists Laboratory Accreditation Program accredits the entire spectrum of laboratory test disciplines with the most scientifically rigorous customized checklist requirements.

The CAP's pear based inspector provides a unique balance of regulatory and educated coaching supported by the most respected worldwide pathology organization.

THE STEPS TO CAP ACCREDITATION

The laboratory seeking accreditation

1. Applies and completes application
2. Receives custom checklists and prepares for inspection
3. The CAP assigns inspector / team assembled
4. Inspection conducted (Three month winder)
5. Corrects cited deficiencies and demonstrates compliances
6. Meets requirements accredited for 2 years
7. Performs a self-inspection at years

Benefits of CAP Accreditation

➢ Meets the Clinical Laboratory Improvement Amendment (CLIA) Regulatory requirement (Specific to laboratories in the US).

- ➢ Ensures compliance through the guidance of the most comprehensive scientifically endorsed laboratory standards.
- ➢ Maintains accuracy of test result and ensures accurate patent diagnosis
- ➢ Increases the value they bring to organizations, customers and patients.

CAP accreditation is available for laboratories conducting tests on human and animals in the US and other countries.

INTERNATIONAL SCENARIO

USA: JCHAO - Discussed earlier

Canada: Canada has the second largest established accreditation program in the world. The Accreditation is done by the Canadian Council on Health Services Accreditation (CCHSA) which is a national, not for profit independent body accrediting the primary, secondary and care services providers nationally and internationally.

France: In France there is the National Agency for Accreditation and Evaluation in Healthcare (ANAES). French Accreditation College (FAC) has been given responsibility for Accreditation.

New Zealand: In New Zealand, Quality Health New Zealand, an independent, not for profit organization is spear heading a voluntary accreditation program for hospitals and health care services.

South Africa: The council on Health Services Accreditation for South Africa (COHSAA) was started as National Collaborative effort between state, private sector consumers and health professionals COHSAA – carried out Accreditation program.

United Kingdom: In UK, the Health Quality Services (HQS) Ireland: In Ireland, the Irish Health Services Accreditation Board

Germany: In Germany an Independent voluntary accreditation program

Malaysia: In Malaysia, the Malaysian Society for Quality in Health (MSQH)

Australia: Please refer to the topic Australian Commission on safety & quality in Healthcare.

Australian Commission on Safety and Quality in Health Care

National Safety and Quality Health Service (NSQHS) Standards drive the implementation of safety and quality systems and improve the quality of health care in Australia.

The commission is a government agency that leads and co-ordinates national improvements in safety and quality.

Clinical Care Standards:

The commission works to formulate and monitor safety and quality standards and work with clinicians to identify best practice clinical care to appropriateness of serious being delivered in a particular health care setting.

- ➢ The health service organizations implement the actions required to meet the NSQHS. Standards and select on approved accrediting agency to assess their compliance in making the NSQHS Standards. This involves a contractual relationship with the accrediting agency that recognises that assessment data will be provided to state and tertiary health departments and the Commission for reporting and review.
- ➢ The approved accrediting agencies assess health service organizations against the NSQHS standards.
- ➢ Then they report to Health Ministry annually on safety and quality.

PRIZES AND AWARDS

Deming's Prize:
- ➢ Established in 1950
- ➢ Awarded by Juse - Japan Union of Scientists and Engineers

Includes 10 points called Deming Prize Check:
- ➢ Policy
- ➢ Organization and operation

- Education and training
- Collecting and using information
- Analysis
- Standardization
- Control
- Quality assurance
- Effect
- Planning for the factors

European Quality Award:
- Launched in Paris by EFQM - European Foundation for Quality Management.
- Its aim is to recognize organizations who are paying exceptional attention to quality management land to encourage others to follow their example

9 Points Frame work:

Enabling Factors	Result Factors
1. Leadership - 8%	1. People Satisfaction- 9%
2. Policy and Strategy - 9%	2. Customer Satisfaction - 20%
3. People Management - 9%	3. Impact on Society - 6%
4. Resources - 14%	4. Results - 15%
5. Process - 14%	
Total 50%	Total 50%

The Process:
- The applicant has to address all criteria in the report.
- The assessors give scoring by detailed comments.
- The top surer after the first round are subject to site visit.
- There is a detailed code of conduct for the assessors.
- Actual situation compared, and report is submitted to the jury

UK Quality Award:
- Started by British Quality Foundation in 1990
- Awards are given to the organization that achieves control over a comprehensive quality infrastructure and show from
- their TQM effect.
- It offers a frame work for evaluating quality critical elements:
- Quality Improvement Programme
- Customer Care Programme
- Quality Assurance Programme

IMC Ramkrishna Bajaj National Quality Award
- Instituted by the Indian Merchant's Chamber.
- To recognize and promote the importance of quality to competitiveness, productivity and standard of living. There are Three Categories -
- Manufacturing
- Service
- Small scale sector

Criteria:
- Customer oriented quality focus.
- Formulate clearly defined values and inculcate them into their company's operations.
- Well, designed and well executed systems and processes
- Continuous improvement in the management of all systems and processes.
- Develop goals as well as strategically aim to expert their products and services.
- Minimizing the response time for all operations and processes.
- Operations and decisions of the company must be based on
- facts.
- Employees training and involvement in quality improvement action.

- Designing quality and error prevention as key elements of quality systems.
- Communicate quality requirements to support and evaluate performance.
- Values of Shri Ramakrishna Bajaj must form an integral part of executive leadership.
- Plan to create an impact on society in the areas of education of women, women's welfare and rural development.
- A Trust comprising of prominent leaders from Indian companies as Trustees has been formed to foster the success of the programme. The trust selects the winners based on the recommendation of a panel of judges.

IMC Juran Quality Medal:
- The award is named after De. Juran – one of the quality Gurus
- This medal is presented annually to an individual who has contributed to enhancing the quality image of India.

Ten Criteria:
- Outstanding leadership in establishing customer driven quality.
- Outstanding leadership in combining statistical thinking and management which results in high quality of products and services.
- Outstanding leadership in improving the supplier aspects of quality.
- Outstanding leadership in improving the human aspects of quality.
- Effective quality management training and/or consulting in the manufacturing of service and small-scale sectors.
- Successful design development and making of quality management publication, books and instruction system.
- Substantial original research on the processes, tools and techniques for quality in
- Substantial original quality management research that has social significance.
- Promotion of awareness through articles conventions and other means.

- Distinct philanthropy dedicated to promotion of quality management
- The process of evaluation involves inviting three external judges.

Golden Peacock National Quality Award (GPNQA)
- Named after India's national bird 'Peacock'.
- Awarded every year – for winner and runner up

Categories:
LE - Large Enterprises - > 251 employees ME – Medium Enterprises - 51-250"

SE - Small Enterprises - Up to 50"

Special Categories:
1. Education, Training, Research and Development, Testing and Inspection
2. Service Sector, covering Tourism, Transport, Couriers, Hotels and Hospitality, Health care, Telecommunication, Professional Consultants, Financial Institutions
3. Government organizations, undertakings and Services

Eligibility:
- Operations of applicant most reasonably correspond to all the Award criteria and which can be verified in India at the time of evaluation.
- The application will be assessed and scored on a scale from 0-1000 points using GPNQA Model for Total Quality Management.

Rajiv Gandhi National Quality Award:
- Instituted by Bureau of Indian Standards in 1991.
- To encourage Indian manufacturing and service organizations to strive for excellence and giving special recognition to those, who are considered to be the leaders of quality movement in India.
- Named after Rajiv Gandhi – recognizing the new thrust he had given to the quality movement in India, so that India could more into 21st century with pride.

Objects:

- Encouraging Indian Industry to significant improvement in quality for maximizing consumer satisfaction.
- Recognizing the achievements.
- Establishing guidelines and criteria for quality improvements.

Future Of Quality in Health Care

The world is changing so rapidly that it is difficult to predict what the future would be in any field. This is true about healthcare and quality also. Changes in healthcare are taking place because of several factors, chief among them is technological advances. The relationship among all the stakeholders is altering, especially between doctor and the patient. Doctors are increasingly becoming dependent on technology both for diagnosis and treatment. Patients are becoming well informed and their expectations are increasing. Life style diseases are posing severe challenge. Cost of health care is increasing day by day.

In this scenario the way health care is being delivered and assurance of quality is going to change. It is difficult to imagine how it would be or should be. But we may just foresee of some trends.

To meet the challenges of technological advancement, increasing patients' expectations and cost escalation, quality will be in focus more than what it is today.

Quality in preventive care is going to be very vital because that area is going be given prominence by the health care providers especially the government and nongovernment agencies. The change is going to be more from Health Care to Health Creation.

In one of the meetings to consider the future of quality some experts opined that:

- There is going to be Flip - sudden movement and swift changes Listen to patients - what they really want (Today, we offer them what we think what the patient needs but not necessarily what they want). To provide what patient wants and needs is quality of the future.
- One has to raise the bar. The level has to reach the directors, trustees and high officials to be involved in quality.
- There should be collaborative care Role of social media is going to play a major role in quality of health care. The providers have to be sensitive to the feedback of the patients, relatives and friends. Perhaps following are going to be trends which require modifications in quality assurance.

- Increased patients' expectations.
- Patient's rights will have more focus.
- Technological advancement: Role of support services,
- especially, biomedical department to ensure quality outputs.
- Standardization - both in clinical and non-clinical areas.
- Increasing regulatory controls
- More focus on providing quality healthcare in a cost-effective way
- Litigations may increase - necessitating provision of evidence based quality care.
- Insurance companies may play major role and insist on accreditation for all the health care organizations, where insured patients are utilizing the services.

Improving quality to reduce medical errors decrease the costs – by eliminating all forms of wastes is going to be Mantra in future.

If the mode of diagnosis and treatment itself changes – because of newer developments, like stem cell, therapy, genetic engineering and immunotherapy the healthcare delivery may change and the set ups for quality assurance and management may have to change but the basic principles will remain same.

References

1. Alderwick H, et al. Making the case for quality improvement: lessons for NHS boards and leaders. King's Fund, 2017.

2. Alzolibani A. A. (2011). Patient satisfaction and Expectations of the Quality of Service of University Affiliated Dermatology Clinics.Journal of Public Health and Epidemiology, 3(2), 61–67.

3. Antony, J., Palsuk, P., Gupta, S., Mishra, D., & Barach, P. (2017). Six Sigma in healthcare: a systematic review of the literature. International Journal of Quality & Reliability Management, 35(5), 1075-1092.

4. Aryankhesal A. Strategic Faults in Implementation of Hospital Accreditation Programs in Developing Countries: Reflections on the Iranian Experience. Int J Health Policy Manag. 2016;5(9):515–517. doi: 10.15171/ijhpm.2016.70.

5. Asch SM, Kerr EA, Keesey J, Adams JL, Setodji CM, Malik S, McGlynn EA. Who is at greatest risk for receiving poor-quality health care? N Engl J Med. 2006 Mar 16;354(11):1147-56. doi: 10.1056/NEJMsa044464. PMID: 16540615.

6. Asif, M., Jameel, A., Sahito, N., Hwang, J., Hussain, A., & Manzoor, F. (2019). Can leadership enhance patient satisfaction? Assessing the role of administrative and medical quality. International Journal of Environmental Research and Public Health, 16(17), 3212.

7. Ayeleke RO, North N, Wallis KA, Liang Z, Dunham A. Outcomes and impact of training and development in health management and leadership in relation to competence in role: a mixed-methods systematic review protocol. Int J Health Plann Manage. 2016;5(12):715–720.

8. Bamidele A. R. Hoque M. E. Heever H. V. (2011). Patient Satisfaction with the Quality of Care in a Primary Health Care Setting in Botswana.South African Family Practice, 53(2), 170–175. 10.1080/20786204.2011.10874080.

9. Bradley E, Hartwig KA, Rowe LA. et al. Hospital quality improvement in Ethiopia: a partnership-mentoring model. Int J Qual Health Care. 2008;20(6):392–399. doi: 10.1093/intqhc/mzn042.

10. Chakraborty, S., & Gonzalez, J. (2018). An integrated lean supply chain framework for U.S. hospitals. Operations and Supply Chain Management, 11, 98–109.

11. Chakraborty, S., Kaynak, H., & Pagán, J. A. (2021). Bridging hospital quality leadership to patient care quality. International Journal of Production Economics, 233, 108010.

12. Cleveland EC, Dahn BT, Lincoln TM, Safer M, Podesta M, Bradley E. Introducing health facility accreditation in Liberia. Glob Public Health. 2011;6(3):271–282. doi: 10.1080/17441692.2010.489052.

13. Conn CP, Jenkins P, Touray SO. Strengthening health management: experience of district teams in The Gambia. Health Policy Plan. 1996;11(1):64–71. doi: 10.1093/heapol/11.1.64.

14. Coskun, S., & Gulhan, Y. Ts EN 15224 Healthcare Service-The Comparison of Quality Management System to Other Quality Systems in Healthcare. Research Journal of Business and Management, 4(3), 410-416.

15. Dahlgaard, J. J., Pettersen, J., & Dahlgaard-Park, S. M. (2011). Quality and lean health care: A system for assessing and improving the health of healthcare organisations. Total Quality Management and Business Excellence, 22(6), 673–689.

16. Das J, Mohpal A. Socioeconomic status and quality of care in rural India: new evidence from provider and household surveys. Health Aff (Millwood). 2016; 35 (10): 1764 – 73.

17. Department of Health (DH) High quality care for all: NHS Next Stage Review final report. London: Department of Health; 2008.

18. Dimovska D, Sealy S, Bergkvist S, Pernefeldt H. Innovative pro-poor healthcare financing and delivery models. Washington, DC: Results for the Development Institute; 2009.

19. Dixon-Woods M, Baker R, Charles K, Dawson J, et al. Culture and behaviour in the English National Health Service: overview of lessons from a large multimethod study. BMJ Qual Saf. 2014;23:106–115. doi: 10.1136/bmjqs-2013-001947.

20. Dixon-Woods M, McNicol S, Martin G. Ten challenges in improving quality in healthcare: lessons from the Health Foundation's programme evaluations and relevant literature. BMJ Qual Saf 2012;21:876-84. 10.1136/bmjqs-2011-000760.

21. Donabedian A. Health Administration Press; Ann Arbor: 1985. Explorations in quality assessment and monitoring. Vol. I. The

definition of quality and approaches to its assessment, 1980; Vol. II. The criteria and standards of quality, 1982; Vol. III. The methods and findings of quality assessment and monitoring: an illustrated analysis.

22. Donaldson, M. S. (2008). An overview of To Err Is Human: Re-emphasizing the message of patient safety. In R. G. Hughes (Ed.), Patient safety and quality: An evidence-based handbook for nurses, advances in patient safety. Agency for Healthcare Research and Quality (US).

23. Estiri M. Heidary Dahooie J. Zavadskas E. K. (2023). Providing a Framework for Evaluating the Quality of Health Care Services Using the HealthQual Model and Multi-Attribute Decision-Making Under Imperfect Knowledge of Data.Informatica (Vilnius), 34(1), 85–120. 10.15388/23-INFOR512.

24. Finkelstein JA, Brickman AL, Capron A, et al. Oversight on the borderline: Quality improvement and pragmatic research. Clin Trials 2015;12:457-66. 10.1177/1740774515597682.

25. Finley FR, Ivanitskaya LV, Kennedy MH. Mentoring junior healthcare administrators: a description of mentoring practices in 127 US hospitals. J Healthc Manag. 2007;52(4):260–269.

26. Healthcare Quality Improvement Partnership A guide for clinical audit, research and service review — An educational toolkit designed to help staff differentiate between clinical audit, research and service review activities. HQIP, 2011.

27. HealthGrades, Inc. (2008). HealthGrades quality study: Fifth annual patient safety in American hospitals study. AHRQ.

28. Hillman T, Roueche A. Quality improvement. BMJ Careers 2011;342:d2060 10.1136/bmj.d2060.

29. Hughes, R. G. (2008). Tools and strategies for quality improvement and patient safety. In R. G. Hughes (Ed.), Patient safety and quality: An evidence-based handbook for nurses. Agency for Healthcare Research and Quality.

30. Institute of Medicine (IOM) Crossing the quality chasm: a new health system for the 21st century. London: IOM; 2001.

31. Jha, A. K., John Orav, E., Li, Z., & Epstein, A. M. (2007). The inverse relationship between mortality rates and performance in the hospital quality alliance measures. Health Affairs, 26(4), 1104–1110.

32. Johnston G, Crombie IK, Davies HT, Alder EM, Millard A. Reviewing audit: barriers and facilitating factors for effective clinical audit. Qual Health Care 2000; 9:23-36. 10.1136/qhc.9.1.23.

33. Kebede S, Abebe Y, Wolde M, Bekele B, Mantopoulos J, Bradley EH. Educating leaders in hospital management: a new model in Sub-Saharan Africa. Int J Qual Health Care. 2010;22(1):39–43. doi: 10.1093/intqhc/mzp051.

34. Khanna T, Rangan VK, Manocaran M. Narayana Hrudayalaya Heart Hospital: cardiac care for the poor (A). Cambridge (MA): Harvard Business School; revised 2011 Aug. (Harvard Business School Case 505-078).

35. Kwamie A, Dijk Hv, Agyepong I. Advancing the application of systems thinking in health: realist evaluation of the Leadership Development Programme for district manager decision-making in Ghana. Health Res Policy Syst. 2014; 12:29. doi: 10.1186/1478-4505-12-29.

36. Ladhari R. (2008). Alternative measures of service quality: A review.Managing Service Quality, 18(1), 65–86. 10.1108/09604520810842849.

37. Le H-G, Ehrlich JR, Venkatesh R, Srinivasan A, Kolli A, Haripriay A et al. A sustainable model for delivering high-quality efficient cataract surgery in southern India. Health Aff (Millwood). 2016 ; 25 (10): 1783 – 90.

38. Leatherman S, Sutherland K. Designing national quality reforms: a framework for action. Int J Qual Health Care. 2007;19(6):334–340.

39. Lee P.M., Khong P., Ghista D.N., Mohammad MosadeghRad A. The impact of organizational culture on the successful implementation of total quality management. TQM Mag. 2006;18(6):606–625.

40. Mandeep, Chitkara N., Goel S. Study to evaluate change of attitude toward acceptance of NABH guidelines: an intra-institutional experience. J Nat Accred Board Hosp Healthcare Providers. 2014;1:52–55.

41. McDonald KM, Sundaram V, Bravata DM, Lewis R, Lin N, Kraft S et al. Technical Review 9: Closing the quality gap: a critical analysis of quality improvement strategies: volume 7—care coordination [Internet]. Rockville (MD): Agency for Healthcare Research and Quality; 2007 Jun [cited 2016 Aug 22]. (AHRQ Publication No. 04[07]-0051-7).

42. McLaughlin, C. P., McLaughlin, C., & Kaluzny, A. D. (2004). Continuous quality improvement in health care: Theory, implementation, and applications. Jones and Bartlett.

43. McNicholas C, Lennox L, Woodcock T, Bell D, Reed JE. Evolving quality improvement support strategies to improve Plan-Do-Study-Act cycle fidelity: a retrospective mixed-methods study. BMJ Qual Saf 2019;28:356-65. 10.1136/bmjqs-2017-007605.

44. Mohanad Halaweh, Fathi Fayeq Salameh, Using Social Media Data for Exploring Healthcare Service Quality, International Journal of Healthcare Information Systems and Informatics, 10.4018/IJHISI.325064, 18, 1, (1-13), (2023).

45. Mohanan M, Bauhoff S, La Forgia G, Babiarz KS, Singh K, Miller G. Effect of Chiranjeevi Yojana on institutional deliveries and neonatal and maternal outcomes in Gujarat, India: a difference-in-differences analysis. Bull World Health Organ. 2014; 92 (3): 187 – 94.

46. Morton M, Nagpal S, Sadanandan R, Bauhoff S. India's largest hospital insurance program faces challenges in using claims data to measure quality. Health Aff (Millwood). 2016; 35 (10): 1792 – 99.

47. Nabitz, U., Klazinga, N., & Walburg, J. (2000). The EFQM excellence model: European and Dutch experiences with the EFQM approach in health care. European Foundation for Quality Management. International Journal for Quality in Health Care, 12(3), 191–201.

48. Nelson, C. W., & Niederberger, J. (1990). Patient satisfaction surveys: An opportunity for total quality improvement. Hospital and Health Services Administration, 35(3), 409.

49. Parasuraman A. Zeithaml V. A. Berry L. L. (1988). SERVQUAL: A Multiple-Item Scale for Measuring Consumer Perceptions of Service Quality. [doi:NA]. Journal of Retailing, 64(1), 12–40.

50. Rathee M. Quest for quality: pivotal paradigm for healthcare transformation. J IDA North West Delhi Branch. 2016;3(2):55–56.

51. Reed JE, Card AJ. The problem with Plan-Do-Study-Act cycles. BMJ Qual Saf 2016;25:147-52. 10.1136/bmjqs-2015-005076.

52. Rosen, M. A., DiazGranados, D., Dietz, A. S., Benishek, L. E., Thompson, D., Pronovost, P. J., & Weaver, S. J. (2018). Teamwork in healthcare: Key discoveries enabling safer, high-quality care. American Psychologist, 73(4), 433–450.

53. Rowe LA, Brillant SB, Cleveland E. et al. Building capacity in health facility management: guiding principles for skills transfer in Liberia. Hum Resour Health. 2010;8:5. doi: 10.1186/1478-4491-8-5.

54. Sarto F, Veronesi G. Clinical leadership and hospital performance: assessing the evidence base. BMC Health Serv Res. 2016;16 Suppl 2:169. doi: 10.1186/s12913-016-1395-5.

55. Schuster, M.A., McGlynn, E.A., and Brook, R.H. How Good is the Quality of Health Care in the United States? Milbank Q 76:517-563, 1998.

56. Schwarcz SK, Rutherford GW, Horvath H. Training for better management: avante Zambezia, PEPFAR and improving the quality of administrative services: Comment on "Implementation of a health management mentoring program: year-1 evaluation of its impact on health system strengthening in Zambezia province, Mozambique" Int J Health Policy Manag. 2015;4(11):773–775. doi: 10.15171/ijhpm.2015.136.

57. Shenoy A, Revere L, Begley C, Linder S, Daiger S. The Texas DSRIP program: An exploratory evaluation of its alignment with quality assessment models in healthcare. Int J Healthcare Manage. 2017;12(2):165–72.

58. Shenoy, A. Patient safety from the perspective of quality management frameworks: a review. Patient Saf Surg 15, 12 (2021). https://doi.org/10.1186/s13037-021-00286-6.

59. Sikka R, Morath JM, Leape L. The Quadruple aim: care, health, cost and meaning in work. BMJ Qual Safety. 2015;24:608–10.

60. Smits HL, Leatherman S, Berwick DM. Quality improvement in the developing world. Int J Qual Health Care. 2002;14(6):439–440. doi: 10.1093/intqhc/14.6.439.

61. Spath, P. (2014). Introduction to Healthcare Quality Management (Vol. 2). Chicago. IL. Health Administration Press.

62. Taylor MJ, McNicholas C, Nicolay C, Darzi A, Bell D, Reed JE. Systematic review of the application of the plan-do-study-act method to improve quality in healthcare. BMJ Qual Saf 2014;23:290-8. 10.1136/bmjqs-2013-001862.

63. Temin M. Learning from disappointment: reducing the cost of institutional delivery in Gujarat, India. In: Glassman A, Temin M, editors. Millions saved: new cases of proven success in global health. Washington (DC) : Center for Global Development ; 2016.

64. The Institute of Medicine Committee on Quality of Health Care in America. Crossing the quality chasm: A new health system for the 21st century. Washington, DC: National Academies Press (US); 2001.

65. Trivedi AN, Matula S, Miake-Lye I, Glassman PA, Shekelle P, Asch S. Systematic review: comparison of the quality of medical care in Veterans Affairs and non-Veterans Affairs settings. Med Care. 2011 Jan;49(1):76-88. doi: 10.1097/MLR.0b013e3181f53575. PMID: 20966778.

66. Vashdi, D. R., Bamberger, P. A., & Erez, M. (2013). Can surgical teams ever learn? The role of coordination, complexity, and transitivity in action team learning. Academy of Management Journal, 56(4), 945–971.

67. Wang H, Liddell CA, Coates MM. et al. Global, regional, and national levels of neonatal, infant, and under-5 mortality during 1990-2013: a systematic analysis for the Global Burden of Disease Study 2013. Lancet. 2014;384(9947):957–979. doi: 10.1016/S0140-6736(14)60497-9.

68. Warren C, Abuya T, Obare F. et al. Evaluation of the impact of the voucher and accreditation approach on improving reproductive health behaviors and status in Kenya. BMC Public Health. 2011;11:177. doi: 10.1186/1471-2458-11-177.

69. Willis-Shattuck M, Bidwell P, Thomas S, Wyness L, Blaauw D, Ditlopo P. Motivation and retention of health workers in developing countries: a systematic review. BMC Health Serv Res. 2008;8:247. doi: 10.1186/1472-6963-8-247.

70. Zepeda, E. D., & Sinha, K. K. (2016). Toward an effective design of behavioral health care delivery: An empirical analysis of care for depression. Production and Operations Management, 25(5), 952–967.

www.ingramcontent.com/pod-product-compliance
Lightning Source LLC
LaVergne TN
LVHW061543070526
838199LV00077B/6885